Selected

EVELYN SCHLAG was born and rai[...]
Lower Austria where she now l[...] German and
English Literature at the Universi[...] of Vienna, and was a teacher
before becoming a full-time writer. She is the award-winning
author of seven volumes of prose fiction, a book of essays on liter-
ature and medicine which reflects her interest in Katherine
Mansfield, and five collections of poetry. She has translated
Douglas Dunn, Mark Doty, Gwyneth Lewis and John Burnside
into German.

KAREN LEEDER is a Fellow and Tutor in German at New College
Oxford. She has published widely in modern German literature,
and has translated Bertolt Brecht, Michael Krüger, Brigitte
Oleschinski and Raoul Schrott.

EVELYN SCHLAG

Selected Poems

translated by Karen Leeder

with an introduction by Evelyn Schlag

CARCANET

First published in Great Britain in 2004 by
Carcanet Press Limited
Alliance House
Cross Street
Manchester M2 7AQ

The publication of this book was supported by the Sektion für
Kunstangelegenheiten, Bundeskanzleramt, Vienna

Poems from *Brauchst Du den Schlaf dieser Nacht* © Paul Zsolnay Verlag,
Vienna, 2002

Poems from *Das Talent meiner Frau* © Residenz Verlag,
Salzburg–Vienna, 1999

Poems from *Der Schnabelberg* were first published by S. Fischer Verlag,
Frankfurt am Main, 1992 © Evelyn Schlag

Poems from *Ortswechsel des Herzens* were first published by S. Fischer
Verlag, Frankfurt am Main, 1989 © Evelyn Schlag

All German poems reproduced by kind permission

Translations and preface © Karen Leeder 2004
Introduction © Evelyn Schlag 2004

A CIP catalogue record for this book is available from the British Library
ISBN 1 85754 652 0

The publisher acknowledges financial assistance from
Arts Council England

Typeset by XL Publishing Services, Tiverton
Printed and bound in England by SRP Ltd, Exeter

Contents

aus *Der Schnabelberg* (1992) /
from *The Schnabelberg* (1992)

aus *Ortswechsel des Herzens* (1989) /
from *Heart Changing Places* (1989)

Translator's Preface

My involvement in this volume originated in a bilingual reading tour of seven UK cities with the Austrian writers Raoul Schrott and Evelyn Schlag and the translator Iain Galbraith, in March 2001. Although I had read some of Evelyn Schlag's work before that in an academic context, the commission to translate a selection of her poems for presentation in a number of poetry venues and university departments across the country brought her poetry alive to me in a new way. That frantic week on the road, hearing and reading the poems, discussing the business of translation every evening, brought a very powerful sense of Evelyn Schlag's voice and inspired me to translate more of her work. I was struck time and again by the music of her poetry and the humane, empathetic spirit that was at work in the German.

This volume contains poems from her early collections up to the volume of selected poems published in Germany in 1999, *Das Talent meiner Frau* (*My Wife's Talent*). But it also includes an extensive selection from her remarkable 2002 collection, *Brauchst du den Schlaf dieser Nacht* (*Do You Need This Night's Sleep*). The poems thus span almost a decade and give a good sense of the poet's development: from the elusive mythological texts to the immediacy and magic of her late Lisbon poems. What is quite clear in her work is a constant interrogation of the shapes we make in the world and what we might pass on of them. These are poems of love and memory then, of erotic intensity and quiet reflection but also, acutely, of loss. There is a wistful melancholy to Schlag's work. And it would not be going too far, I think, to say that a good many of her poems are elegies of one sort or another. It is no chance that one of her most significant achievements as a translator is her versions of Douglas Dunn's *Elegies* (1991). Readers coming to her for the first time will notice the many luminous – but always fractured – landscapes her poetry conjures: from Austria to Portugal, Eastern Europe, the United States and beyond. Also striking is the way a world made animate urgently seeks to communicate, to make itself understood, even as it is threatened by silence, cold and solitude: 'the hastening the freezing night'. What is perhaps easier to miss on a first reading is the playful variety of voices at work in her poetry – some very far from the conventional English canon – the political veracity, but also the humour of her work.

Such a range of poems inevitably presents very different kinds of challenges to the translator: from the dense, unpunctuated early texts with their elusive and slippery syntax and elemental vocabulary, to the quiet authority of her sonnet sequences, or the deceptive limpidity of the 'Summer Elegies'. The overriding constant in Schlag's poetry, though, is a precise attentiveness to architecture and rhythm. I have aimed to follow the energies and the contours of the German as closely as possible while, as every translator must, allowing the poems to find an independent life in a new language. Some of the poems fell quite naturally into English; others were more resistant to their new medium. In these cases I was lucky enough to have the chance to work together with Evelyn to test out with her the images, rhythms and movements of the German. That kind of dialogue emboldened me to make occasional changes to syntax and idiom which I hope render the English versions more faithful to the initial impulse of the German and to the wider demands of poetry itself. The fact that this first selection of Evelyn Schlag's poetry in English is presented in a bilingual format encourages this kind of attention to the spirit of the poetry, and of course it will allow readers to make their own judgement on the success of such an undertaking.

Acknowledgement is due to those who commissioned translations, or otherwise sponsored the original tour which led to work on this volume: the National Touring Program of Arts Council England; the Goethe Institute, London; the Austrian Institute, London; the Warden and Fellows of New College, Oxford; the Faculty of Medieval and Modern Languages, University of Oxford; the Poetry Café, London; the Centre for Creative Writing and the Department of German at the University of Warwick; the British Centre for Literary Translation at UEA; the Poetry Library in Edinburgh; the German Department at the University of St Andrews and the German Department at the University of Aberdeen.

Karen Leeder, 2004

Introduction

The first poetry that struck me with a force I had never experienced before was Paul Celan's. I was fortunate in having a rather unusual German teacher during the last three years of secondary grammar school, a young woman who used to enter our classroom with three or four books under her arm, always including some contemporary literature of the late 1960s. Since I grew up in a conservative little town, it was unusual to become acquainted with Celan and Goethe on equal terms, as it were, and to treasure those brightly rainbow-coloured Suhrkamp paperbacks as much as the *West-Östlicher Divan*.

There was a sense of an enormous freedom and dignity that the German language had regained with poets such as Günter Eich, Hans Magnus Enzensberger, Paul Celan. It was the hermeticism of Celan and, later on, of Ilse Aichinger in particular, that shaped my idea of what poetry should be like. In hindsight it seems that I took from them a licence to efface myself in words and to let language perform and act in my stead. My very first published poems are full of secret meanings, second guessings and dream-like, bizarre characters who claim to know things and talk about them with modernist mannerisms.

I had also, very early on, fallen in love with Rilke. One of the two sequences that make up my volume *Ortswechsel des Herzens* (1989) is called 'Orpheus, Feminine'. It has a strong impulse to address the (beloved) person and shows a concern with perspective and specific voice. These have become characteristic features of my poetry. The title poem ascribes to the voice an almost unlimited power but does so in language that comes close to stammering, hampered by doubt and scruples in finding the right word:

> For you I would sell my
> would sell my self go
> to the good or even the bad
> shepherd judge commandant
> I would use my voice
> to say I have moved mountains
> as he counts out the ransom
> would set you free, set you loose
> until my tongue breaks my voice
> would do that my voice which you
> always hear differently from me

It is this belief (and wanting to believe in this belief) that language, poetry, can move mountains (and that mountains should be moved) that later on drew me to Marina Tsvetaeva. I began reading her in 1988, when I had already finished *Ortswechsel des Herzens*. The second sequence of that volume consists of eighty-four love poems, each of seven lines. I called them 'Septemtriones', constellations of seven stars which have to stand in as a means of communicating with a distant lover. They were written within a couple of months. Not long into the process, the poems demanded that I should organise the matter in six, seven or eight lines – in other words, they should be rather short. That length fitted precisely with what I was able to encompass at the time, given the uncertain nature of the love affair. Everything could come to an end within the short span of seven lines. Again, there is reference to the voice that must sustain that love and the strategies that the poetic voice and the Self adopt:

> Only a handful of words each time
> for me to keep you hungry
> my predator paws bigger than
> my heart – that's how I'd like to be
> encaged claws padded bars with
> every heartbeat running into your
> stay with me.
>   (XXVI)

I have always been drawn to women writers who were forced to write from within a difficult isolation. In the case of Marina Tsvetaeva, the cruelty of her fate was extreme. But her suicide in Yelabuga in 1941 was preceded by a vitality which is hard to match. Take the utter lack of moderation of her demand, 'I gently shake your hand and expect miracles from you', written to an absent devotee: you understand what it means to love. If you read this quietly, and quietly take it seriously, it loses its monstrousness, its hyperbole. For me Tsvetaeva is the poet of the much-longed-for encounter that never takes place.

A woman poet who is as demanding, and as lonely, as Tsvetaeva is the exceptional Austrian poet Christine Lavant (1915–73), who wrote about God: 'Lord I know you searched for me/Even while I was in my mother's womb'. Hers is a radical reproof to God and the almighty power that he abuses; since it comes from the mouth of the unempowered, it is all the more radical. Her poems continually grapple with the Catholic God who, she declares, has disappointed her to the bone – or so it seems. If you read the poems as existential blame hurled at her married lover, the painter Werner Berg, almost every line shines in a wholly new light. Like Tsvetaeva, she never speaks to an audience, but always to an individual.

In a recent essay on the radicalism of Christine Lavant and the Protestant poet Catharina Regina von Greiffenberg (1633–94), I traced similarities between these women. Some of their traits are important for my own writing as well, such as the urge to read nature for signs and messages from 'God', to find out what parallel language may be encoded in nature and its phenomena. Then there is the striking (and seemingly abstract) sensuality in their writing, a corporeal presence that works as a mind opener once you start taking their metaphors literally. It is remarkable what they do with metaphors of the body. Addressing a Yellow Rider, Lavant writes, 'You have to strap me tightly to your back/ But then my heart would be too close.' Her poems sit behind us in the saddle and we feel their heartbeat at our back. Here is the Baroque poet Catharina Regina von Greiffenberg on Jesus Christ: 'I let him swing me, throw me, catch me, as he likes.'

Taking words literally, especially in idiomatic phrases, has from the beginning been one of the cornerstones of my writing. I use it mostly in short, lyrical poems. Quite often these poems have a female speaker who is invested with a sceptical voice, a dry humour regarding male concepts of love, as in 'Fishblood':

> I would have swum up any river
> For his sake just like the fairytales
> That is how he caught me in his wake
> Always five notes ahead the very five
> That I had taken into my head
> And scarcely was I lying on his wet board
> When a voice said if the sunlight
> Falls into the smokehouse the
> Braces glitter like ingots of gold

I was alerted to the fact that a newly renovated castle twenty miles from where I live in Lower Austria had been the home of Catharina Regina von Greiffenberg. I immersed myself in her work and biography and wrote a novella about her. I came to admire her unshakable belief in her mission as a (Protestant) religious poet in intensely hostile Counter Reformation surroundings.

It was only when I translated Douglas Dunn's *Elegies* that I considered rhyme as a serious possibility in my German verse. The sonnet sequence 'Temptations' in my volume *Der Schnabelberg* (1992) positions rhyme in places where you would not expect it in a sentence. It makes rather free use of enjambement. Rhyme, which had a bad reputation in twentieth-century German verse, has remained rare in my poetry, but I have recently tried it again in poems about America that partially use English words to rhyme with German ones, usually in an ironic though playful manner.

A different strand, more narrative in form, has run alongside the tighter, shorter lyric poems. I first used it with political poems and then moved on to express intimate things with it, for example in the long poem about a married couple's sarcophagus in the Etruscan Museum in Rome in *Das Talent meiner Frau* (1999). At the time I was experimenting with a prosody and syntax that would allow for a more relaxed flow without diminishing the weight of content. I have always read widely in contemporary British and American poetry. I discovered Elizabeth Bishop as a teacher. I believe it was her stoicism that influenced poems like 'I have always wanted to live by the sea' and 'The Teddy Bears', while the trembling transparency of Louise Glück's prose poems helped me to find the voice for pieces about marital love, for example the 'Summer Elegies', in my latest volume, *Brauchst du den Schlaf dieser Nacht* (2002). Elizabeth Bishop also supplied the key to the structure of my latest novel *Das L in Laura*. 'Everything only connected by "and" and "and"' became the governing principle for the lofty, gentle network of poems and poets that populate the novel. The poems I wrote in order to constitute an *œuvre* for the main character turned into the sequence of 'Laura's Songs'.

There is something strange about the fact that the story of one's own poetry becomes tellable; what has seemed like a string of hardly related, accidental turns make a sense, almost a plot. It is a story about a search, a search for a Self, the lyrical Self.

Evelyn Schlag, 2004

aus

Brauchst du den Schlaf dieser Nacht

from

Do You Need this Night's Sleep

Elegien eines Sommers

I

Als es vorige Nacht über unseren Bäumen
So anhaltend blitzte und ich immer wieder
Wie ein Reh in die Scheinwerfer lief hast du
Um mich zu beruhigen weitergeschlafen hast
Mit deinem ganzen Körper gesagt bleib ruhig
Und ich habe es dir endlich geglaubt so
Wie du mir glaubtest daß es einen vierten
König gegeben hat und ihn suchtest mit mir
Und als wir ihn gefunden hatten so sicher
Von ihm erzähltest zu den Freunden

II

Tags in diesem Sommer
Verlasse ich dich
In meine Hand gestützt
Ich laufe in die offenen Arme
Und Bücher eines Mannes der
Mit allen seinen Sinnen schreibt
Mir mehrmals am Tage schreibt

Ich erzähle ihm von einer Fahrt
An die Moldau im Januar
Als wir mit einem Freund
Das gefrorene Herz des Flusses
Suchten unter gestautem Wasser
Das alte Flußbett das
In einem anderen Weiß gefriert

from *Brauchst du den Schlaf dieser Nacht*

Summer Elegies

I

Last night when the lightning split the sky
For hours above our trees and I kept running
Like a deer into the headlights you
Slept on undisturbed to calm me said
With your whole body stay calm
And in the end I believed you just like
You believed me when I said there had been
A fourth wise man and looked for him with me
And when we had found him told the story
With such certainty to your friends

II

These summer days
I leave you
Head propped on my hand
I run into the open arms
And books of a man who
Writes with all his senses
Writes to me several times a day

I tell him about our journey
To the Moldau in January
Setting out with a friend
To find the frozen heart
Of the river under the halted
Water the old river bed which
Freezes to a different white

Und wie wir es endlich sahen
Seine Konturen nachzeichneten
Mit ausgestreckten Armen
In der eisigen Luft
Geschichte von der ich wußte
Ich würde sie jemandem erzählen

Ich erzähle sie einem Mann
Der mich liebt und ich bin dir
Auf eine unbekannte Art treu so
Als hätte ich noch genauer gelernt
Dich richtig zu lieben

Und es ist deine Hand die ich
Im nächsten Moment erkenne
Die mich hält wenn ich erwache
Am späten Nachmittag dieses
Um Ewigkeiten zu kurzen Sommers

III

Ich trieb im Meer in Reichweite
    Meiner Lektüre und sah
        Deine Arme weit ausholen

Und es war noch einfach
    Einem Fremden zuzuwinken
        Der auf der schwimmenden Insel

Weiter draußen stand und
    Aussah wie du wenn du im
        Aufbruch bist und wie immer

Wenn du gehst sah ich
    Auf die Uhr und begann zu
        Zählen vergaß dich eine Weile

Oder dachte an dich nur
    In Bildern wie du nachts
        Deinen Arm schwer über mich

from *Brauchst du den Schlaf dieser Nacht*

And how we saw it at last
Traced its contours
With our arms stretched out
In the icy air
A story I knew I would
One day tell someone

I tell it to a man
Who loves me and in a strange
Way it is not a betrayal as if
I had learned a more exact way
Of loving you truly

And the next moment I see
That it is your hand that
Holds me as I awake
In the late afternoon of this
Summer that was ages too short

III

I drifted in the sea within reach
    Of my books and saw
        Your arms lifted for the stroke

And it was still easy enough
    To wave to a stranger
        Who was standing further away

On the floating jetty and
    Looked like you when you
        Are about to leave and as usual

When you go I looked
    At my watch and began to
        Count forgot you for a while

Or thought of you only
    In pictures how at night
        You lay your heavy arm

Legst und ich innerhalb und
   Außerhalb deines Schlafs bin
      Wie du die Beute die so viele

Worte für das Entkommen hat
   Behältst trieb und suchte
      Wieder und war mir ganz sicher

Diese zwei Fische außerhalb
   Der Bojen die um einen Sprung
      Versetzt miteinander zur anderen

Küste tanzen das bist du
   Trieb so lange so lange im
      Kreis und hinaus und quer und

Immer wenn ich Grund hatte
   Hüpfte ich um dich zurückkommen
      Zu sehen und als ich nach zwei

Stunden aus dem Wasser ging
   Allein sah ich dich ins Wasser
      Gehen auf der Suche nach mir

IV

In der Renaissancestadt Ferrara wo ich
Alles vergaß dreimal englische Bücher
Kaufte wo kleine Hunde und Palmbäume
Im Radfahrerkorb vor dem Volant sitzen

Und ein Palast steht der die Langeweile
Vertreibt wo im verdorrten botanischen
Garten eine Eidechse sich sonnte über zwei
Senfbraune Schafgarben gestreckt die nicht

Auseinandertrieben wie unsere Hotelbetten
Wo vor dem Dom alte Männer stehen an ihr
Rad gelehnt mit den Taschen von Boutiquen
Und die Frauen auf dem Rad telefonieren

from *Brauchst du den Schlaf dieser Nacht*

Across me and I am inside
    And outside your sleep
        And you hold the prey which has

So many words for escape
    Captive I drifted and searched
        Once more and was quite sure

That those two fishes beyond
    The buoys only a stroke apart
        And dancing together to a distant

Coastline were really you
    I drifted so long went so long
        In circles and out and astray

And every time I found my feet
    I floated up to see you coming
        Back and after two hours

When I came out of the water
    I saw you going in alone
        In search of me

IV

In the Renaissance town of Ferrara where I
Forgot everything bought English books
Three times where people ride with little dogs
And palm-trees in their bicycle baskets

And where there's a palace to while away the empty
Afternoons where in the parched botanical
Garden a lizard was sunning itself stretched
Across two mustard-brown yarrow leaves which

Didn't move apart like the beds in our hotel
Where in front of the cathedral old men pause
Lent on their bikes with their fancy carrier bags
And the women ride past chatting on their mobiles

from *Do You Need This Night's Sleep*   7

In Ferrara in dessen Zentrum du uns mit
Einer einzigen alle Schilder mißachtenden
Cowboydrehung brachtest sagtest du zu mir
Ich habe dich noch nie Rad fahren gesehen

V

Du erzähltest wie du als kleiner Junge
Beidhändig am Glockenseil zogst
Strenge Stimmen im Ohr
Die nie ein Tier sprechen ließen

Ich erzählte dir vom Schulweg hielt mir
Meinen geköpften Zopf ans Genick
Der in Seidenpapier gehüllt schläft
Ich war einmal ein blondes Kind

Jeder aus seinem Schlaf kommend
Griffen wir am Morgen zugleich
Nach des anderen Hand wie es uns
Beim Tanzen nur selten gelingt

VI

Heute plätschert die Sonne
Wie damals in den ersten Stunden
Des Tages herum zerfließt und
Verfließt sich über die Wiesen
Egal ob dort Schafe sind

Junge Schafe Kälber kleine Spinnen
Kleine Maulwürfe Tiere die als Junge
Fast schon so groß wie Alte sind
Mit Schnauzen die einen Millimeter
Wachsen Maß einer Lebenserfahrung

　　　　　from *Brauchst du den Schlaf dieser Nacht*

In Ferrara in the centre of town where you
Brought us with a single cowboy swerve
Ignoring every road-sign you said to me
I have never seen you riding a bike

V

You would tell how as a little boy
You tugged on the bell-rope with both hands
Stern voices ringing in your ear
That never made animals speak

I told you how I went to school held
My beheaded plait that now sleeps safely
Wrapped in silk paper against my neck
I was once a blonde-haired child

As we surfaced from sleep that morning
We reached out and found each other's
Hand – something we seldom manage
When we are dancing

VI

Today the sun is splashing
The light like once before in the first
Hours of morning it smears and
Smudges itself across the fields
Regardless of sheep

Lambs calves little spiders
Young moles animals where the young
Are almost the size of the adults
With snouts that grow only a millimetre
The measure of a lifetime's experience

Wir werden nur dir und mir
Gegenüber alt nicht im Blick
Zu aufschießenden Kindern was
Ist es das man von uns erwartet

Wir sind immer erst kurz
Verheiratet als hätten wir uns
Spät kennengelernt nach allen
Fehlern und wüßten besser als
Die anderen was Liebe ist Liebe
Nur zwischen zweien die
Immer im vollen Licht stehen

VII

Wer ähnelt uns? Wer wiederholt
Unseren Gang über abgerissene
Felder wo die Schnittstellen
In den Himmel starren? Wer macht
Unsere Zeichen nach verzieht
Aufmerksam die Lippen um ein Wort
So zu sprechen wie wir? Was fehlt
Wenn wir keinem etwas vorsprechen
Können und fehlt etwas? Stirbt
Die Sprache aus? Gehen Wörter
Zugrunde wenn du mir den Arm
Um die Hüfte legst solange du willst?

VIII

Wenn ich dir sage die Landschaften in
Fremden Gedichten sehen immer größer aus

Freier – „jener erste Winter in Wiltshire"
Das dehnt die Bedeutung der Felder weit

from *Brauchst du den Schlaf dieser Nacht*

We only grow old in the eyes of
Each other not in those of the children
Who shoot up taller every day what
Is it that people expect from us

It always feels we have only just
Married as if we had found
Each other late after all
The mistakes and knew better than
The rest what love is the love
Of two people who always stand
In the full light of day

VII

Who will take after us? Who will one day
Stroll the way we strolled across the
Emptied fields where the open cuts stare
Blankly at the sky? Who will make
The signs we made patiently shape
Their lips to say a word
The way we do? What is missing
When there's no one to read our lips
And is there anything missing? Does
Language die out? Do words
Fall away when you rest your arm
Round my hips for as long as you want?

VIII

When I tell you the landscapes in
The poems of others always seem bigger

Freer – 'that first winter in Wiltshire'
It gives the fields a meaning that stretches

Zurück in alle vergangenen Jahrhunderte
Wenn ich dir sage ich lerne so langsam ich

Brauche Jahre um unsere Landschaft zu sehen
Sagst du *Es ist wie mit allem was man liebt*

Jahrelang anschaut diese dunklen Berge die
Uns gehören sich jeden Abend anders zu den

Hinter ihnen liegenden verhalten es ist so
Mit dir es ist so mit den Alpen deren Gewicht

Wir hier gerade noch spüren wo die Obstbäume
Schäumen im Mai und denk an die vielen Ernten

Denk an deine schwarzgekleidete Person die ich
Auch in Schwarz noch immer nicht zeichnen kann

IX

Wir gehen in die Jahreszeit wenn sie
Noch nicht gekommen ist wir reden
Schon lange vorher von ihr mit Ängsten
Als müßten wir den schwarzen Morgen lang
Über die Felder geistern auf der Suche
Nach dem Beginn des Lichts

Wir streichen mit dem Finger über
Feuchte Bretter schauen verwundert
Unsere gespreizte Kinderhand an
Als wäre es eine von vielen noch zu
Entdeckenden Membranen mit denen
Sich die Welt überzieht

from *Brauchst du den Schlaf dieser Nacht*

Way back century upon century
When I tell you I am such a slow learner

I need years to learn to see our landscape
You say *That's the way with everything one loves*

And watches for years these dark mountains
We call our own that every evening seem to sit

Differently against those behind it's like that
With you it's like that with the Alps whose weight

We sense even here where the fruit trees
Are froth in May and remember the many harvests

Remember your figure dressed in black
Which I still cannot draw even in black

IX

We inhabit the season long
Before it arrives we speak of it
For months tell all our fears
As if we had to haunt the fields
Through the long dark of morning
And search for the start of light

We stroke our fingertips across
Damp boards stare in wonder at
Our hand spread out like a child's
As if it were one of the many
Membranes still to be discovered
The skins that clothe the world

Wir gehen in die Übung der Jahreszeit
Die Türen schließt wissen daß wir uns
Einmal an eine Tür lehnen die nachgibt
Aber uns hält leichter als wir jemals
In den Blick eines Liebenden trieben
Leichter als wir die gelben Früchte
Auf dem Baum in die Hand wogen

Augenblick ohne Zeitmaß in dem wir
Uns verwandeln in das Gedächtnis
Des Felswegs den wir so oft gingen
Gedächtnis der jahrhundertealten Bilder
Gedächtnis von Menschen die mit uns
Unter der Sonne standen und noch
Unter der Sonne stehen Zahl
Die immer kleiner werden wird

X

Heute nacht spielte der Kater
Mit der Gürtelschnalle deiner Hose
Und ganz leise versuchte ich es
Ihm auszureden heute nacht als
Der Kater über unsere Kopfkissen
Schlich erzählte ich ihm daß du
Gestern den steilen Berg hinauf
Nicht vom Rad steigen mußtest
Nebel Nieselregen in dem du dich
Zum gebräunten Freund umdrehtest
Und wie wir den Freund lieben wenn
Er zur Wohltat des Hierseins nickt
Augen kurz geschlossen so als
Hätte ich nicht nur gekocht für uns
Sondern die Welt so gemacht wie sie ist
Wenn sie gut ist Farben der Pilze
Schlieren des Weins und der wilde Wein
Der mit Beerenkronen wie ein Pfau
Auf der Balkonbrüstung zittert

from *Brauchst du den Schlaf dieser Nacht*

We school ourselves in the season
Of closed doors know that one day
We will lean against a door that gives
But holds us more gently than ever
We bathed in the gaze of a lover
More gently than we cradled
The yellow fruits on the tree

A moment without measure the moment
In which we change into the memory
Of the cliff path we so often walked
Memory of the centuries-old pictures
Memory of the people who stood with us
Under the sun and still stand
Under the sun a number
Which gets smaller every day

X

Last night I found the tomcat playing
With the belt-buckle on your trousers
And I tried very quietly to talk him
Out of it last night when I saw him
Creeping across our pillows I told him
That yesterday you stayed on your bike
All the way up the steep slope
Mist sleet and you turning
Back to our sun-tanned friend
And how we love this friend
When he nods with pleasure at being here
His eyes shut for a moment as if
I had not simply cooked for us
But had made the world the way it is
When it is good the colours of mushrooms
The legs of the wine and the wild vine
That trembles with crowns of berries
Like a peacock on the balustrade of the balcony

Wir stehen weit hinten
Im Park des Hauses
Das uns nicht gehört
In dessen vielen Zimmern
Die Sonne den Tag lang
Mit Flecken an der Wand
Mit immer neuen toten
Fliegen spielt

Wir stehen hinter den Astern
Die uns mit ihren ersten
Violetten Punkten sagen
Der Sommer ist gebrochen

Wir stehen hinter der Kapelle
Mit den Bänken für Gliedmaßen
Aus einer anderen Zeit

Wir stehen im lange
Stillgelegten Gemüsegarten
Mit Zackensteinen eingefaßt
An denen entlang du das Gras
Wie englischen Rasen mähst

Dort wo vor fünfzig Jahren
Die Dienstboten sich bückten
Stehst du hinter mir ziehst
Mir den Rock hoch und
Die Wäsche hinunter

XI

We are standing far away
In the grounds of the house
Which is not ours
Where all day long
In the many rooms
The sun plays
On the bare stained walls
With more and more dead flies

We are standing beyond the asters
That tell us by their first
Violet button-heads
That summer has broken

We are standing behind the chapel
With its pews carved for limbs
Of a different age

We are standing in the old
Abandoned vegetable garden
With its border of little stones
And you mow the grass to the very edge
Like a perfect English lawn

On the spot where fifty years ago
The servants stooped to work
You stand behind me pull
My skirt up round my waist
My underwear to my feet

XII

Du bist eingeschlafen ins Fauteuil
Geschmiegt Beine über der Armlehne die
Weißen Kliniksocken zum schwarzen Gewand
Dieser *unverzeihliche Fehler* des guten
Geschmacks Kopf in zwei Finger gestützt
Die andere Hand hält halb eingerollt
Eine Kunstzeitschrift es flackern über
Deine Wange Überlegungen du bereitest
Eine Entscheidung vor von der ich nichts
Weiß die mich umso gewisser betrifft und
Deine geschlossenen Lippen sagen auf eine
Weise Nein wie nie im Wachsein als hätten
Sie es von dem letzten Seher gelernt im
Ofen rücken die Scheiter zurecht geben
Laute der Erleichterung von sich

XIII

Wir stehen in walisischem Regen die Schafe
Ziehen auf parallelen Pfaden über den Hang
Wo der Nachbar im Juni beim Heumachen niest

Hundertachtzig Grad weiter übt eine kleine
Blasmusik abends über Felder Graben Felder
Bis zu uns wir hören den blechernen Hund

Gleich daneben die Rehböcke gegen den Mond
Wenn der Staub des Motocross zurückgesunken ist
Jedes Korn an einem anderen Platz als zuvor

Wir hören die Privatsprache des Bussardpaars
Nach dem wir uns die Köpfe verrenken wir
Hören hörst du das? Die Marder im Dachboden

Das sich anpirschende Auto über dem Kies
Das wieder kehrtmacht David Krakauers Sax
Aus der Speisekammer wenn ich koche

from *Brauchst du den Schlaf dieser Nacht*

XII

You have dozed off curled up in the armchair
Legs flung over the arm revealing
White hospital socks beneath your black suit
An *unforgivable lapse* in good taste
Head resting on two fingers the other hand holding
An art magazine which slowly unrolls as thoughts
Flicker across the muscles of your cheeks
You are moving towards a decision of which I know
Nothing which is all the more certain to be about me
And your closed lips say no in a way
They never do when you're awake as if
They had learned it from the last visionary
In the oven the logs settle themselves
Giving off little sounds of relief

XIII

We are standing in Welsh rain the sheep
Follow the parallel paths across the hill-side where
Our neighbour sneezes during haymaking in June

Turn through one hundred and eighty degrees and
The evening practice of a brass band drifts across fields
Ditches fields we hear the tinny yelp of the dog

And close by the deer roaring at the moon
When the dust of the motorbikes has settled again
Every speck in a different spot from before

We hear the secret talk of a pair of buzzards
Which we crane our necks to catch we hear
Do you hear it? The martens in the attic-space

The car stalking its way across the gravel
Then turning round David Krakauer's saxophone
From the larder when I'm cooking

from *Do You Need This Night's Sleep*

Wir hören die Grillen und nur ich höre
Die Fliege bei Nacht wir hören das Kratzen
Des Katers an der Tür in Akkorden von drei

Oder vier wir hören seit es Krieg gab weniger
Flugzeuge den Schüttelfrost des Kühlschranks
Wir hören den farblosen Ton des Computers

Und hören keinen Straßenlärm und ich
Zähle das auf gegen meine Angst daß du
Taub werden wirst so wie ich halbblind

XIV

Für den einen Tag unseres Sommerfests
Kehrt der Sommer zurück mit Tischen
Im Gras und bunten Tellern aus dem Land
In dem wir alle geboren sein wollen

Anstatt in den Schatten der Alpen und
Du suchst mit Gerhard der mich Kochen lehrte
Die Weine aus für zehn Gänge von Mittag
Bis in die Nacht wenn wir mit Decken sitzen

Mittag bis in die Nacht feiern wir vier Paare
Vor verfallender Kulisse daß wir uns kennen
Salzen nach verwöhnen den Hund den
Der Kater von weit her im Gebüsch fürchtet

Zwei waren zu weit im Süden um die Finsternis
Mitten am Tag erlebt zu haben den Anmarsch
Des Untergangs genau wie im Religionsbuch
Unserer Kindheit so daß wir ihm glaubten und

Für kurze Zeit danach alles wie gezeichnet
Aussah und es zu jedem nur einen anderen gab
Und wir wußten wenn einer der beiden geht
Wird der andere stumm dunkel kalt

from *Brauchst du den Schlaf dieser Nacht*

We hear the crickets and I alone hear
The fly buzzing at night we hear the cat
Scratching at the door in bursts of three

Or four and since war was declared we hear fewer
Planes the shivering fit of the fridge
We hear the colourless hum of the computer

And hear not a sound from the street and I
Store it all up against my fear that you
Will go deaf and I will become half-blind

XIV

For this one day of our summer feast
The summer returns with tables on the grass
And brightly coloured plates from the country
Where we all wish we had been born

Instead of in the shadow of the Alps and
With Gerhard who taught me to cook you
Are choosing wines for ten courses from midday
Until the early hours when we will huddle in blankets

From midday until the early hours we four couples
Will sit before the crumbling edifice to celebrate our
Friendship add more salt spoil the dog
While the cat skulks at a distance in the bushes

Two of us had been too far south to see
The darkness in the middle of the day the beginning
Of the end exactly like the pictures
In childhood catechisms and we believed it

And for a while everything seemed to be marked out
And everyone was meant for the one they were with
And we were sure if either of us departed
The other would be silent dark cold

XV

Zugezogener Vorhang der zwischen den
Offenen Flügeln am Fenstersims streicht
Wie ein Tanzkleid aus Streifen weiße
Streifen und deine Knie sind vom Radsturz
Unbrauchbar deine Ellbogen aufgescheuert
Es kreischen die Häher weil sie wieder etwas
Vergessen haben und es rufen die Freunde
Die zu früh kommen den Weg des Rehs nehmen
Während du sagst *stütz dich auf über mir* und
Wir uns in Ruhe ganz aus der Ruhe bringen
Die kleinen Dünen Holzstaubs unter dem Schrank

XVI

Als dann an der Westseite des Hauses
Die Astern blühten in acht Farben
Vom Rosa bis ins dunkelste Violett
Und auf einem großen Fleck an der
Südseite in einer einzigen Farbe

Da lief ich viele Male hin und her
Mit diesen jeweils nur Sekunden zurück
Liegenden Eindrücken und konnte nicht
Sagen war es dasselbe Violett wollte
Keine Blüte abschneiden zum Beweis und

Begriff schließlich es kam nicht darauf an
Den absoluten Farbsinn zu haben oder daß
Deine Liebe immer erkennbar sei auch auf
Die Verwunderung mit der ich mich jedes
Mal neu verliebte wenn ich davor stand

Könnte ich mich nicht verlassen nur auf
Die täglich kürzer leuchtende Sonne die
Alle überflüssigen Wörter ausblendet so
Daß die Farben noch zu sich kommen vor
Der beschleunigten und frierenden Nacht

from *Brauchst du den Schlaf dieser Nacht*

XV

The drawn curtain which hangs between
The open shutters brushes the window-ledge
Like an evening dress in swathes of white
And your knees are a mess where you fell
Off your bike your elbows grazed raw
The jays are squawking again after something
They have left behind and our friends are calling
Arriving too early taking the deer-path
Then you say *prop yourself up above me*
And quite calmly we leave all calm behind
The little dunes of wood-dust under the wardrobe

XVI

Then when the asters were in flower
Against the west-wing of the house
In eight shades from pink to darkest mauve
And there was one great patch
On the south side of a single colour

I ran back and forth countless times
With the image of that colour only
Seconds away not wanting to cut
A flower to check but could not say
Whether it was the same mauve

Until at last I understood I did not need
A perfect sense of colour nor always to
Recognise your love nor could I count
On the sense of wonder every time
I fell in love when standing before them

I could only count on the sunlight
That dwindles a little each day
And obscures all the extra words
So the colours come into their own
Before the hastening the freezing night

from *Do You Need This Night's Sleep*   23

Für Stunden vor dem Mond war ich allein
Ich suchte im Garten nach dir wie du dich
An einen Baum lehnst oder mit zwei Fingern
Den stacheligen Zweig aufhebst an einem Blatt

Ich suchte nach deiner Stimme aber die Luft
War leer und durchlässig für alles andere
Ich hatte größte Musikalität und Mühe war müde
Wünschte mir die Wiederkehr einer Erscheinung

Jenseits des Gartens sah ich eine Flut gelben
Löwenzahns sind das noch unsere Gefilde?
Ich hätte es gern an deinem Gesicht abgelesen
Die Schatten ob sie Abdrücke von Liebenden

Oder Sterbenden? Schatten kannte ich eine Art
Fell das ich am Boden schleife bis die Sonne
Nicht mehr brennt aber wozu sind wir berufen?
Was ist das ein Liebender eine Sterbende? Und

Es würde bedeuten daß jemand vor uns hier war
Daß wir uns nach Namen bückten die anderen
Entfallen waren besseren Menschen wirklichen
Ersten Menschen nicht solchen Spielern wie wir

Und hörte dich dann endlich kommen wie du
Die schwere Tür aufdrückst ins Haus mir rufst
Die Tasche auf die Bank wirfst in den Garten
Läufst oder die Treppe hinauf alles zugleich

Sah dein Gesicht das Lachen und Sorge mischt
Seit zum erstenmal du mir entstiegst und
Wir wußten daß wir einmal gehen werden müssen
Weil uns nicht zusteht das Glück der Tiere

from *Brauchst du den Schlaf dieser Nacht*

XVII

For hours before the moon came up I stood
Alone scanning the garden to see you appear
Leaning against a tree or moving aside
A bramble with two fingers holding the leaf

I listened for your voice but the air
Was empty letting everything else crowd in
I had music in me sorrow sleep
Longed for the return of an apparition

Beyond the garden I could see a sea of yellow
Dandelions do those fields belong to us too?
I wanted to be able to read in your face
Whether the shadows there were the imprint of lovers

Or the dying? I knew shadows they weigh heavy
Like a kind of pelt I trail along the floor until
The sun stops burning but what are we called to be?
And what is a lover what a dying woman? And

That would mean that someone has been here before us
That we have stooped to pick up names that someone
Else has lost along the way better people real
First people not charlatans like us

And then at last I heard you coming pushing
Open the heavy front door calling me
Throwing your bag on the bench and running
Into the garden or up the stairs all at once

And I saw your face with its traces of laughter and worry
Since the first time you slipped away from me
And we knew that we would one day have to leave
Because we do not deserve the bliss of animals

Ich wollte immer am Meer wohnen

Als du
Nach meiner Lungenentzündung
Nach Wochen des Hustens sagtest
Ich will mich bald
Wieder auf dich legen

Sah ich mich als Skelett
Eines Schiffs aus leichtem Holz
Auf einem Strand allein
Und spürte mich zersplittern
Unter deinem Gewicht dem Meer

Meine bleichen Planken
Ließen dich über sich ergehen
Verwandelten sich in etwas
Das dem Sand schon sehr ähnlich war

Und es war ein gleichmäßiges Brechen
Unter der Welle deines Körpers
Der gründlich war wie das Meer
So daß kein größeres Stück blieb
Kein Anlaß zur Trauer

from *Brauchst du den Schlaf dieser Nacht*

I Have Always Wanted to Live by the Sea

When
After my pneumonia
And weeks of coughing you said
I want to lie
On you again

I saw myself as the skeleton
Of a ship made of light wood
Alone on a beach
And felt myself splintering
Under your weight the sea

My bleached planks
Let you wash over them
Slowly changing into something
That was almost sand

And there was the constant breaking
Under the wave of your body
Which was thorough like the sea
So that no larger pieces remained
No occasion for grief

Laß uns nicht sagen woher wir kommen

Laß uns vor die Tür gehen vorbei an
Den Tischchen mit der Stimme des Hauses
Vorbei am Patron den Mänteln zum erhobenen
Arm des Küchenmädchens das zum ersten Mal
In diesem Jahrhundert erscheint und draußen
Laß uns den Vorhang zuziehn und es soll
Nacht sein unerklärter Himmel unter dem wir
Einander aus aufgeregtem Herzen Sätze sagen
Die unser Beruf sind die Blicke der Applaus
Der vor dem letzten Wort der Strophe kommt

Laß uns die Hausmauer entlang gehen
Rücken zur gekachelten Wand mit kleinen
Schritten seitwärts die fremde Gasse
Gehen nur an den Fingerspitzen einander
Bestätigend weil sonst die Häuser
Einstürzen die Kirchen wegfliegen mit
Ihren Glocken und Gold und wenn wir unter
Den Gerüchen des Schlafs vorbeisteppen
Weiße Muster aus Marmor unter der Sohle
Dann lehn dich einmal zurück mit mir leg
Den Kopf an das Gemäuer schiel zu mir

Laß uns wieder Platz nehmen nebeneinander
Im Tag im Bus und die Mäntel falten für
Unsere Hände als wären wir die Teenager
Von vor dreißig Jahren laß uns über unseren
Köpfen den Knopf suchen für die frische Luft
Von draußen Hand an Handgelenk spielen wem
Der Wind die Haare verbläst während wir zur
Festung hinaufschaukeln in einem riesigen
Sanften Tier jeder Schritt gleich gebremst
Als habe es selbst Angst vor seiner Wucht

Laß uns die Wäsche zählen nein die Hunde
Die bis vor meine Schuhspitze schlafen
Und was empfiehlst du mir sonst diese
Kirche diesen botanischen Bahnhof ach
Was bin ich froh daß wir keine Simulationen
Sind um ihre eigene Achse insektengrünes

from *Brauchst du den Schlaf dieser Nacht*

Let Us Not Give Away Where We Come From

Let us go outside past the little
Tables with the voice of the house past
The patron the coats the raised arm
Of the kitchen-maid who appears
For the first time this century and outside
Let us draw the curtain and it shall be night
An unexplained sky beneath which we stand
Our hearts fit to burst exchanging sentences
These are what we profess the looks the applause
That comes before the last word of the stanza

Let us walk along the wall of the house
Our backs to the tiles walk sideways
With little steps along the strange alley
Finding each other only with our
Fingertips in case the houses collapse
The churches take off with their bells
And their gold when we
Tap-dance past the smells of sleep
White patterns of marble under our soles
And for once lean back with me lay your
Head against the wall sneak a look at me

Let us choose seats side by side again
In the day in the bus and fold our coats
For our hands as if we were the teenagers
Of thirty years ago let us search for the
Button above our heads for fresh air from
Outside play hand against wrist whose hair
The wind should blow while we are
Bouncing uphill to the fortress in a huge
Soft beast that brakes at every step
As if it were afraid of its own might

Let us count the washing no the dogs
Slumbering right up to the tips of my shoes
And what else can you recommend this
Church this botanical railway station oh
How glad I am that we are not simulations
Turning on our own axis insect-green

from *Do You Need This Night's Sleep*   29

Skelett oder Delphin mit Nacht gefüllt
Die man nicht greifen kann nein sag nichts
Das ist dein Ellenbogen und das ist dein Knie

Laß uns fünfzehn Minuten mehr haben wir
Nicht durch die islamischen Jahrhunderte
Gehen und lies mir lieber nicht den ganzen
Text vor *alma* heißt Seele laß uns mehr
Haben wir nicht nur auf die Lichtstreifen
Des gefilterten Tags steigen wie es der
Plattfüßige Vogel aus Bronze gewiß nicht
Kann o laß uns während die Seefahrer
Draußen älter werden und sich das Halstuch
Weiter knüpfen verlängern auch unsere Frist
Laß unsere durchsichtigen Gesichter in
Der Vitrine denselben Einfall haben ihn
Herausholen auf deinen und meinen Mund
Laß uns Schutz suchen im Ornament und riech
Wie gut das Glanzpapier riecht im Katalog

Laß uns den Turm hochklettern du voran
Die Hand an der Säule bis auch ich die
Lufttritte kann und deine Worte so besorgt
Um jeden Schritt mir nicht mehr in die Bluse
Rutschen laß uns den zwei alten Herren
Begegnen die von oben kommen wir stehen mit
Flachem Bauch ein Lächeln und ein Schirm laß
Uns endlich ausatmen Arm an Arm als dürfe es
Keiner sehen als hätten wir es selbst nicht
Erlebt und läsen es uns zur Überredung vor

Laß uns alle Straßen gleichzeitig zum Fluß
Gehen denn es ist schon das Meer und die
Hummerfühler der roten Brücke bewundern
Die sich der Diktator bauen ließ mein Blick
Nimmt am liebsten die Brücke aber wir versuchen
Es Hand über Hand riskieren mit leichtem
Körper den Absturz als Flug und unser
Letzter Kontakt mit diesseitigem Grund
Muß dann ein Dichter sein auf daß er
Eine neue Datei anlege wir erreichen
Das Ufer in Gestalt persönlicher Fürwörter
Zwei berühmte Verfallene völlig getarnt

from *Brauchst du den Schlaf dieser Nacht*

Skeletons or dolphins filled with night
That one cannot touch no do not say a word
This is your elbow and this is your knee

Let us have fifteen minutes we do not have more
For a walk through the Islamic centuries
And you had better not read out the whole
Legend to me *alma* means soul let us
We do not have more only step on the strips
Of light in the filtered day as the flat-footed
Bird of bronze certainly cannot do
Oh while the seafarers outside are growing
Older tying their scarves more loosely
Let us put off our deadline as well
Let our transparent faces in the glass case
Have the same idea take it out onto your
Mouth and my mouth let us seek shelter
In ornament and will you smell how good
The glossy paper smells in the catalogue

Let us climb up the tower you first
Hand on the column until I too can manage
The steps up into air and your words so concerned
About my every step stop slipping into
My blouse let us encounter the two old gentlemen
On their way down we are standing with flattened
Bellies a smile and an umbrella let us breathe out at
Last arm touching arm as if nobody should see
As if we ourselves had not experienced it and
Were reading it out to convince ourselves

Let us walk down all the streets to the river
At once for here it is already the sea and
Admire the lobster feelers of the red bridge
Which the dictator had built for himself
My favourite view is over the bridge but
Let us try it hand over hand with light
Bodies risk the fall as flight and let our
Last contact with the solid ground of this
World be a poet so that he may start
A new file and we reach the shore
In the shape of personal pronouns two
Famously spellbound minds in camouflage

from *Do You Need This Night's Sleep*   31

Laß uns diesen Zug nehmen nein den
Früheren lauf das Laufband entlang wir
Überholen die Geschichte die du erzählst
Und der erste Waggon ist leer alle Waggons
Sind leer man sieht bis ans Ende der Flucht
Wo mir der Schlaf fehlen wird und du mich
Beschwörst mit deinem Schweigen alles zu
Vergessen die Stationen der Fahrt die Gedichte
Die über der Tür angezeigt werden mit roten
Buchstaben mich beschwörst in deinem Arm

Laß uns den vollbesetzten Bus nehmen die
Serpentinen hinauf rasen zum Königspalast
Stehend weil dein Arm so schön schaukelt
Und der Waldrand zur Seite hüpft laß uns
Das Gleichgewicht tauschen mit genauer Hand
Und fall nicht aus der geschlossenen Tür
Über den Rand der Zeile in Ungesagtes in
Worte die wir füreinander nie haben werden
Weil wir einander nicht haben werden

Laß uns auf dem Zinnengang rund um
Das Schloß gehen wo man nur Wald sieht
Und einmal hier einmal dort einen spitzen
Schöngedrechselten weißen Turm auf einem Haus
Der sich vor uns verneigt uns ein Märchen
Zu Füßen legt wir nehmen es an allen
Stellen auf und laß uns dann im Wind stehen
Die Rollen verteilen du fährst also auf
Deine Insel ich geradenwegs in die Mitte
Des Kontinents getrennte Flüge getrennte
Letzte Einkäufe mit buntem Spielgeld
Plastiktische mit höflich fragenden
Reisenden ob hier noch Platz sei

Laß uns entkommen aus diesem Märchen
Solange wir seine Sprache verstehen und
Deine Insel ans Festland binden wirf ein
Lasso aus dem Buch das du gerade liest
Und zieh dich zu mir ich habe die
Seemänner ausgefragt nach dem Dreh-und
Schlingentanz mit dem sich ein Seil zur Ruhe
Legt und an den Knoten überlies wie meine
Hände bluteten während ich mir Befehle gab

from *Brauchst du den Schlaf dieser Nacht*

Let us take this train no the earlier one
Run down the moving pavement we are
Overtaking the story you are telling us and
The first coach is empty all the coaches are
Empty you can see right through to the end of
The flight where I will be desperate for sleep and
You will beseech me with your silence to forget
Everything all the breaks in the journey the poems
That are displayed over the door in red
Writing you will beseech me in your arm

Let us take the bus crammed to the last seat
Dash up the Serpentine to the royal palace
Standing since your arm swings so beautifully
And the forest's edge hops to one side let us
Exchange our balance with exact hands and
Do not fall out of the closed door off
The end of the line into things unsaid
Into words we will never have for each
Other since we will not have each other

Let us walk on the battlements round the
Castle where you can only see forest
And here and there the pointed finely-
Turned white turret of a house that
Bows down before us lays a fairytale
At our feet we take it up in all places
And let us then stand in the wind distribute
The roles you are going to your island
I'm to go straight to the heart of the
Continent separate flights separate
Final shopping-trips with colourful toy money
Plastic tables with travellers asking
Politely is this seat free

Let us escape from this fairytale while
We still understand its language and let us tie
Your island to the mainland throw a lasso
From the book you are reading and pull
Yourself over to me I have questioned
The seafarers for the turn- and the loop-
Dance that brings a rope to rest
And in the knots please fail to read how my hands
Were bleeding as I gave myself the commands

Laß uns des anderen Hand halten Finger und
Finger sich verabreden wenn wir einander auf
Der Steintreppe begegnen im Wald du herunter
Ich hinauf als hätten wir gelernt aus dem
Sinken und Steigen der zwei Lifte im Hotel
Wo uns ein Schicksal gegeneinander abwog
Laß uns über den Waldboden der maurischen
Ruine gehen durch Räume die niemandes Raum
Mehr sind nichts mehr schützen als einen
Kuß und wir halten ihn nur vor uns selbst geheim

Laß uns nicht sagen woher wir kommen
Keinen Mythos finden für unseren
Ungezeugten Beginn weil nichts uns
Erklärt als was wir schreiben weil wir
Hier nichts als Dichter sind ständig
In Gefahr und im Besitz der Worte laß
Meine Worte die Wange sein deine den Mund
Der gegen sie flüstert die Pause in der
Nur dein Atem warm spricht und wieder
Meine Worte das Weiterflüstern deines
Moments laß uns jeder das Gedicht darin
Hören das sich in ein Gedicht verlieben
Wird Werk das sich verschränkt weil
Alle anderen Schranken überhoch sind

Laß uns den blauen Palast im Notizbuch
Verzeichnen Speicher füllen mit seinen besten
Szenen als hätten wir mit steinernen Knien
Ein Bad genommen im leeren Bassin und laß
Uns auch den Finger legen auf die Scherben
Des Geschirrs das das Fest über seine Schulter
Warf und das jetzt die Wand der Grotte schmückt
Finger auf die Scherben damit auch wir nur
Einmal so getafelt haben laß uns im Schlaf
In Brüche gehen und von fremder Hand zusammen
Gesetzt werden die keinen Unterschied sieht

from *Brauchst du den Schlaf dieser Nacht*

Let us hold each other's hand finger fix a
Rendezvous with finger when we meet on
The stone stairs in the wood you coming down
Me going up as if we had learned the lesson from
The sinking and rising of the two lifts in the hotel
Where a single fate weighed us against each other
Let us walk across the forest floor of the Moorish
Ruins through rooms that are nobody's room any
More that do not safeguard anything but a
Kiss which we keep secret only from ourselves

Let us not give away where we come from
Invent no myth for our unbegotten
Beginning because nothing will explain
Us but what we write because here we
Are nothing but poets forever in
Danger and in the possession of words
Let my words be the cheek yours the mouth
That whispers against it the pause in which
Only your breath speaks warmly and again
My words the next whisper of your
Moment let us each hear the poem within
That will fall in love with a poem
Work crossing over since all other
Barriers are higher than life

Let us note down the blue palace fill
Our memories with its best scenes as if
We had taken a bath in the empty basin
With knees of stone and let us also rest
Our finger on the shards of the crockery
Which the feast threw over its shoulder
And which now adorns the grotto wall
A finger onto the shards so that we too will
Have dined like this only once let us in
Our sleep go to pieces and be reassembled
By the hand of a stranger who sees no difference

aus *Laura's Songs*

Ihr Reiselied

Ich fahre mit dir in den Kalender
  Der jeden Tag eine Reise plant
Nur weil uns der Buchstabe gefällt
  Mit dem Venedig und Vilnius beginnt

Ich reise mit dir in die Stunde
  Die ich dir immer voraus bin
Seit ich verschoben von der Zeit
  Mich etwas früher in dich verliebt

Ich reise mit dir in die Sterne
  Wo sie klein wie Spielzeug sind
Wo wir sie so legen können daß
  Man alle Wege zu Fuß gehen kann

Ich reise mit dir in die Nacht
  In die brennenden Feuer am Hang
Die Unsäglichkeit zweier Körper
  Die diese Liebe erst möglich macht

Ich reise mit dir ins Labyrinth
  Wo es nach Tassos Rosmarin riecht
Wo deine Begierde die Zweige teilt
  Und einen anderen Ausweg sucht

Ich reise mit dir in den März
  Weil du da einmal geboren bist
Tagegleich mit meiner Hündin
  Die ihre Nase in die Sonne reckt

Ich reise mit dir in den Schnee
  Wo die fremden Tiere stehen und
Du ihnen von dem Papagei erzählst
  Und schwörst der Rabe war bunt

from *Brauchst du den Schlaf dieser Nacht*

from *Laura's Songs*

Song of Her Journey

I travel with you to the calendar
    That plans a journey for every day
But only because we both love the letter
    With which Venice and Vilnius begin

I travel with you to the hour
    That I am always ahead
And displaced by time I was
    The first of us to fall in love

I travel with you to the stars
    Where they are small as toys
Where we arrange them so that
    Everything can be reached on foot

I travel with you into the night
    The burning fires on the hill
And two unimaginable bodies
    That make possible this love

I travel with you to the labyrinth
    With its smell of Tasso's rosemary
Where your desire parts the twigs
    And looks for another way out

I travel with you into March
    Since you were born there once
On the same day as my dog
    Who stretches her nose into the sun

I travel with you to the snow
    To see the strange animals stand
And you tell them of your parrot
    And swear the raven was coloured

Ich reise mit dir ins *Rembrandt*
  In deine Bar mit dem alten Bild
Wo die Männer sich gern verlieben
  Und die Männer auf der Suche sind

Ich reise mit dir in die Bücher
  Wo es uns schon hundertmal gibt
Wo wir einander zitieren und
  Das allerletzte Wort haben wir

Wenn sie über ihn hinwegfliegt

Du weißt noch wie ich flog
  Über London nach Washington
Mein Herz war ein Kolibri
  Genau über deiner Stadt

Du hattest keine Zeit mich
  In die Arme zu nehmen doch
Wir telefonierten flüsternd
  Und nah ohne Landesvorwahl

Du beschriebst mir die Streifen
  In deinem neuen schwarzen Hemd
Mit dem Finger fuhr ich sie nach
  - - - - vor Sehnsucht blind

Deine Stadt war beleuchtet
  Ich sah dich mit Chaucer
Im Gespräch auf dem Balkon
  Er hatte den Mantel abgelegt

Das sah ich und auf dem Monitor
  Liefen die Daten über uns
Soviele Fuß über deinem Dach
  Durch das es im Dezember tropft

Eine unsichtbare Kinderhand
  Dreht das weiße Flugzeug
Auf dem Bildschirm von dir weg
  Todernst wie im Kinderspiel

from *Brauchst du den Schlaf dieser Nacht*

I travel with you to the *Rembrandt*
   Your bar with the old Dutch portrait
Where men like to fall in love
   And men are on the make

I travel with you to the books
   Where we appear a hundred times
Where we quote one another and
   Always have the last word

As She Flies Over Him

You remember a while ago
   I flew via London to Washington
My heart was a hummingbird
   Right over your town

You didn't have time
   To take me into your arms
But we phoned close as a whisper
   Without the international code

You described the stripes
   In your new black shirt
I traced them with my fingertip
   To - - - - blind with desire

Your town was illuminated
   I saw you with Chaucer
Conversing on your balcony
   He had taken off his coat

I saw this while the information
   Appeared on the monitor
So many feet above your roof
   Which every December leaks

An invisible child's hand
   Turns the white plane
Away from you on the screen
   In deadly earnest like a child's game

Ich lese die Meilen pro Stunde
Ich verlasse dich viel zu schnell
Mein Herz ist ein Kolibri
Genau über deiner Stadt

Ihr Chicago Blues

Ich stand am todsicheren Fenster
Meines Hotels in Chicago
Die Plastikkarte für mein Zimmer
Meine codierte Zukunft in der Hand

Ich zählte die tausend Zahlen
Bis hundert ich wußte wie
Ich dich nennen sollte und
Wie mein Leben weiterging

Ich dachte an die junge Frau
Im Sears Tower 103. Stock
Die auf einer Bank saß
Den Blick tief in sich versenkt

Gab es irgendwo eine Philosophie
Jene größeren Ideen die tagein
Tagaus mit Horizonten verhandeln
Der Farbgebung riesiger Wälder

Ich sah dem Motorradfahrer zu
Schritt für Schritt zurücktänzelnd
Parkte er seine Maschine ein
Befreite beidhändig seinen Kopf

Gab es nicht etwas Konkretes um dir
Die gestohlenen Pferde zu zeigen
Dich aus dem Sattel zu holen
Wenn du mich verlassen willst

Ich wollte am Fenster stehen wenn
Du meinen Vornamen umarmst
Wenn du deine Arme um meinen
Immer kühlen Nacken legst

from *Brauchst du den Schlaf dieser Nacht*

I read the miles per hour
    I am leaving you much too fast
My heart is a hummingbird
    Right over your town

Her Chicago Blues

I stood at the jump-proof window
    Of my Chicago hotel room
The plastic key-card
    My encoded future in hand

I counted the thousand digits
    To one hundred I knew
By which name I should call you
    And how my life would go on

I thought of the young woman
    (Sears Tower, Floor 103)
Sitting there on a bench
    Absorbed in her own thoughts

Was there a philosophy
    Those definitive ideas that day in
Day out negotiate with horizons
    The palette of giant forests

I watched the motorcyclist
    Dancing backwards step by step
He parked his engine and
    Freed his head with both hands

Wasn't there something concrete
    I could do to show you the stolen
Horses and lift you down from
    The saddle before you could leave

I wanted to stand at the window
    When you embraced my first name
Putting your hands around
    My neck that is always cold

Ihr nüchternes Lied

Die Trinker am Bahnhof in Brüssel
    Erwarten ans Geländer gelehnt
Die schönsten Szenen der Oper
    Niemand wartet so wissend wie sie

Mit den Armen auf der Stange
    Die Mäntel weit offen die Hände
Lose wie zum Gebet verschränkt
    Warten sie auf Cecilia und Bryn

Als ich am Tag nachdem du fuhrst
    Wieder durch den Bahnhof ging
Zitterten ihre Hände schneller
    Weil sie dachten du kämst zurück

Ihre Augen waren noch gerötet
    Von der vergangenen Nacht
Als du mir das Versprechen gabst
    We shall meet again soon

Die Trinker am Bahnhof in Brüssel
    Sahen mir zu wie ich es glaubte
Als du es schon nicht mehr glaubtest
    Auf der Stufe allein in den Waggon

Einem wird die Luft zu trocken
    Einer steckt den Kopf in den Mantel
Als warte er auf die Verwandlung
    Der traurigen Heldin in ein Lied

Wenn sie ihm etwas aufträgt

Liebster halt dein Auto an
    Eine Zeile hüpfender Blätter
Überquert die Straße im Wind
    Auf und ab zu meinem Lied

Her Sober Song

The drunks at the station in Brussels
    Are waiting at the balustrade
For the highlights of the opera
    Nobody waits as expert as they

Their elbows rest on the railing
    Their coats are wide open their hands
Loosely folded as if in prayer
    They wait for Cecilia and Bryn

On the day after you'd left
    When I returned to the station
Their hands trembled faster
    For they thought you would come back

Their eyes were still reddened
    From the night before
When you gave me a promise
    We shall meet again soon

The drunks at the station in Brussels
    Were watching as I believed it
When you already did not
    On the step of your carriage alone

One of them finds the air too dry
    One tucks his head in his coat
As if waiting for the transformation
    Of the sad heroine into a song

When She Gives Him a Task

Dearest stop your car
    A line of leaves is hopping
Across the road in the wind
    To the rhythm of my song

Ich habe aufgeschrieben was du
　　Mir bringen sollst ins enge Tal
Chaucer und Shakespeare Ovid
　　Das Glas aus dem du trinkst

Einen Picknickkoffer aus Leder
　　Von deiner Bootsfahrt im Bois
Den mit den Schlaufen an der Wand
　　Wohin man Erinnerungen steckt

Bring genug Petrarkismus
　　Für Augen Handgelenk und Mund
Und daß es von mir bis zu dir
　　Nur einen halben Meter weit ist

Eine Schürze mit Fragezeichen
　　Damit ich deine schnellen Sätze
In schönen Bögen langsam
　　Auf die Leine hängen kann

Mangos und Bitterschokolade
　　Die neue Tate den Sainsbury Wing
Und ein Buch in dem ich dir
　　Einen Walzer reservieren kann

Bring alle Kosenamen die du
　　Mir jemals geschrieben hast
Pussycat und *duck* und *my queen*
　　Und vergiß deine Radiostimme nicht

Wenn sie träumt daß er ihr etwas aufträgt

Liebste schreib uns einen Ort
　　Mit einem Balkon aus Stein
Wohin wir abends gehen wenn
　　Der Tag geschlossen ist

Unter dem Balkon aus Stein
　　Müssen Schwäne vorüberziehen
Diskret mit geducktem Kopf
　　Wenn ich dir schöne Dinge sag

　　　　from *Brauchst du den Schlaf dieser Nacht*

I have listed what you should
    Bring to this narrow pass
Chaucer and Shakespeare Ovid
    The glass from which you drink

A picnic hamper made of leather
    From your boat ride in the Bois
One with straps along its sides
    Where we can tuck our memories

Bring enough Petrarchisms
    For my eyes wrist and mouth
And let it be just a matter of
    Two feet from me to you

An apron with question marks
    So I may slowly peg
Your hasty sentences
    Into lovely curves on the line

Mangoes and dark chocolate
    Tate Modern and the Sainsbury Wing
And a notebook where I can
    Save a waltz for you

Bring all the pet names you've
    Ever given me in the mails
Pussycat and *duck* and *my queen*
    And don't forget your radio voice

When She Dreams He Gives Her a Task

Dearest write a place for us
    With a balcony of stone
Where we can go at night
    When the day has closed

Under the balcony of stone
    Swans should come gliding by
Their heads discreetly bowed
    When I whisper sweet nothings

from *Do You Need This Night's Sleep*

Laß es Schwäne sein und das Meer
 Das Meer am besten sehr tief
Damit ich dich bewahren kann
 Vor einem Sprung ins kalte Blau

Nimm die Drums das Akkordeon
 Saxophon Maultrommel und Baß
Als vierte Wand unseres Zimmers
 Die gibt allen Wünschen nach

Dann Liebste zieh den Vorhang vor
 Damit uns keiner dabei sieht
Wie das große Bett der Liebe
 Sich gerade zwischen uns teilt

Gib mir deine Hand damit du
 Nicht weiter von mir treibst
Und hörst du mich denn noch?
 Deine Hand ist weiß ist taub

Liebste schreib wie beschlafen
 Und erwacht von meinem Ton
In dem du alles sagen kannst
 Und den du nun verlierst

Ihr betrunkenes Lied

Manchmal liegt auf den Weiden
 In Wales ein totes Schaf
Die überlebenden Tiere zählen
 Die Stunden bis jemand kommt

Leg den Kopf an meine Schulter
 Du bist so weit so weit
Ich trinke mich betrunken bis
 Du durch dieses Zimmer gehst

Manchmal liegt das Seepferd
 Nova Scotia auf dem Bauch
Speit mit seinem Feueratem
 Ganz Cape Breton aus

from *Brauchst du den Schlaf dieser Nacht*

Let there be swans and the sea
   And the sea shall be deep
So that I can safeguard you
   From leaping into the blue

Take the drums the accordion
   Saxophone Jew's harp and bass
For the fourth wall of our room
   It caves in to every wish

Then dearest draw the curtains
   So that nobody can watch
As this large bed of love divides
   Between the two of us

Give me your hand so you
   Won't drift any further off
And can you hear me still?
   Your hand is white and deaf

Dearest write as if charmed by sleep
   And awakened by my tone
In which you can say anything
   And which you are losing now

Her Drunken Song

Sometimes an old sheep lies
   Dead in a pasture in Wales
The surviving animals count the hours
   Till someone will arrive

Put your head on my shoulder
   You're so far so far
I am going to get drunk
   Till you walk through this room

Sometimes the seahorse Nova
   Scotia is lying on its belly
Spewing out the whole of Cape Breton
   With its fiery breath

Leg den Kopf an meine Schulter
  Du bist so weit so weit
Ich trinke mich betrunken bis
  Du durch dieses Zimmer gehst

Manchmal hab ich dich im Kopf
  In der Schläfe im Nordnordwest
Und wenn ich mich zu dir dreh
  Drehst du dich mit mir um

Leg den Kopf an meine Schulter
  Du bist so weit so weit
Ich trinke mich betrunken bis
  Du durch dieses Zimmer gehst

Manchmal höre ich dich schweigen
  Und dann seufzen doch das ist
Der Drucker der so innehält
  Und tiefen Atem holt

Leg den Kopf an meine Schulter
  Du bist so weit so weit
Ich trinke mich betrunken bis
  Du durch dieses Zimmer gehst

Als er sie besuchen kam

Ich hörte dich sagen das also ist
  Das Haus diese Adresse berühre
Ich Tag für Tag hier liest du mir
  Jedes Wort von den Lippen ab

Ich hörte dich sagen hier also
  Kaufst du den Ingwer für deine
Briefe an mich hier also machst
  Du im Winter die Nacht zum Tag

Dies also ist dein halber Mond
  Der deine rechte Hand bescheint
Hier ist das Grab deiner Hündin
  Über das die gefällte Birke fiel

from *Brauchst du den Schlaf dieser Nacht*

Put your head on my shoulder
   You're so far so far
I am going to get drunk
   Till you walk through this room

Sometimes you're in my head
   In my temple north-north-west
And when I turn around to you
   You turn around with me

Put your head on my shoulder
   You're so far so far
I am getting myself drunk
   Till you walk through this room

Sometimes I hear when you're silent
   And then when you sigh but it's
The printer that has stopped
   And pauses to draw breath

Put your head on my shoulder
   You're so far so far
I am going to get drunk
   Till you walk through this room

When He Came Visiting

I heard you say so this is
   Your house the address that
I touch every day here you lip-
   Read every one of my words

I heard you say so here is
   Where you buy the ginger for
Your letters to me where in winter
   You turn night into day

So this is your half of the moon
   That shines on your right hand
This is the grave of your dog
   Where the birch tree fell

Das also ist dein toter Vater
   In diesem Bach stand das Kind
Blickte nach links nach rechts
   Und wurde traurig wie ein Poet

Ich hörte dich sagen hier also
   Hütest du unser Geheimnis
Auf einer Lichtung ohne Zaun
   In einer Sprache ohne Punkt

Ich hörte im Dunkeln dich sagen
   Diese Hügel strecken hinter
Ihrem Haus nachts die Pfoten aus
   Hier kommt sie am Morgen zu sich

Ich hörte dich sagen hier also
   Suchtest du nach einem andern
Wort als ich mein Wort nicht
   Hielt dich nicht besuchen kam

Wenn sie am Verhungern ist

Schreib mir einen Brief mit der
Hand ich möchte sehen wie du
Meinen Namen schreibst – das L
In Laura ob es eckig ist oder rund

from *Brauchst du den Schlaf dieser Nacht*

So this is your dead father
    In this river stood a child
Looking to the left and the right
    Growing sad like a poet

I heard you say so this is
    Where you keep our wild secret
In a clearing with no fence
    In a language with no stop

I heard you say in the dark
    These hills behind her house
Stretch out their paws at night
    Here she wakes at dawn

I heard you say so here is
    Where you looked for a different
Word when I did not keep mine
    When I did not come visiting you

When She Is Starving

Write me a letter by hand
    I want to see how you
Write my name – the L in Laura
    Whether it elbows or loops

New York 1999

Beim Anflug auf Manhattan
War ich gerührt über
Das steinerne Volk
Das zu mir heraufblickte
Als käme ich vom Mond

Ich dachte an den Vater
Der hier vom Schiff ging
Für mehr als ein Jahr
Um die Kunst der Betäubung
Von Grund auf zu lernen

Ich dachte an die Mutter
Vor die Wahl gestellt
Ihm Briefe zu schicken
Ins Land der vielen Frauen
Oder mit ihm zu fahren

Weil sie das zweite nahm
Lernte ich schreiben
Den Kater auf dem Schoß
Mit seinem gepunkteten Bauch
Schrieb ich immer nur ihr

Was hätte ich ihm erzählen
Sollen ins weiße Hospital
Als er bei der Geburt
Von Caroline Kennedy
In der dritten Reihe stand?

Viele Jahre später schrieb
Er mir zwei Briefe
Ich wohnte auf dem Land
Hatte zwei freundliche Schafe
Mit Namen Susan und Sonntag

Ich habe ja auch Schafe
Schrieb er mir aber leider
Muß ich ihnen die Knie
Brechen lassen das
Versetzt sie in Schock

from *Brauchst du den Schlaf dieser Nacht*

New York 1999

Flying into Manhattan
I was moved
By the stone folk
Staring up at me as if
I were from the moon

I thought of my father
Who disembarked here
And stayed over a year
To learn the art of anaesthetic
From start to finish

I thought of my mother
Having to choose whether
To write letters to him
In this country of many women
Or to travel with him

Because she did the second
I learned to write
With the cat on my lap
Stroking his spotted belly
And always wrote for her

What could I have told him
Busy in the white hospital
And able to stand in the third
Row at the birth of
Caroline Kennedy?

Many years later
He wrote me two letters
I lived in the country
Had two friendly sheep
Called Susan and Sontag

I also have sheep
He wrote but I'm sorry
To say I have to break
Their legs and that
Sends them into shock

Notizen

für Ch. S.

Bei Sonnenaufgang fährt der *Slavija*-Expreß
Durch die Vororte von Belgrad
In den bleichen braunen Maisstangen
Sitzen Elstern und die Kälte der Nacht
Ein Schwarm dieser Vögel fliegt mit
Und eine Krähe überholt sie alle
Ihr Flügelfutter leuchtet auf
In fremden Farben von Rot und Gold

Entlang der Bahn klappernde Slums
Hütten aus oftmals gewendetem Autoblech
Eine Dorfstraße mit Pfützen in der ein Hahn
Hin- und herläuft mit gesenktem Kopf

Halbfertige Lagerhallen oder
Schon verlassene Fabriksgebäude
Im Gras Ziegel da und dort Schutthaufen
Betonbruchstücke wie Ränder von Keksteig

Ein Mann und eine Frau überqueren
Die erste Einfallsstraße in die Stadt
Vier Spuren es fährt noch kein Auto
Kopftuch Mantel im Knöchel gebundene Hosen
Der Mann in Sweater und Jeans er schiebt
Einen leeren Einkaufswagen der bockt

Es ist Oktober neunundachtzig
Der Serbische Schriftstellerverband
Lädt zum 26. Internationalen Kongreß
Im Gedenken an das Amselfeld
Werden auch die Gäste ermuntert
Über das Hauptthema zu referieren
Die Niederlage in Geschichte und Literatur

from *Brauchst du den Schlaf dieser Nacht*

Notes

For Ch. S.

At sunrise the *Slavija*-Express is rushing
Through the suburbs of Belgrade
In the pale brown maize stalks
Sit magpies and the cold of the night
A swarm of these birds keeps pace
With the train but a crow overtakes
Them all the inside of its wing glinting
With strange colours of crimson and gold

The whole length of the track stand rickety slums
Shacks made of recycled scrap car metal
A village street with puddles and a cock
Strutting back and forth with bowed head

Half-finished warehouses or
Factories already abandoned
Bricks in the grass here and there piles of rubble
Lumps of concrete like crusts of pastry

A man and a woman crossing
The first access road into the town
Four lanes still no car to be seen
Scarf coat trousers tied at the ankle
The man in a sweater and jeans pushing
A shopping trolley that lurches and bucks

It is October nineteen-eighty-nine
The Serbian Writers' Union
Greets guests for its 26th congress
In memory of the Battle of Amselfeld
The guests are invited to speak
On the central theme of the conference
Defeat in History and Literature

Im Hotel lächeln die Kellner weich
Schrieb ich beim Frühstück in mein Notizbuch
Und auf dem Spaziergang durch die Stadt
Kaufte ich mir ein übergroßes Adreßbuch
Sonnenblumengelb mit cyrillischem Register
Und weil ich es nicht entweihen wollte
Trug ich keinen Namen ein so daß jetzt
Kein Name einen toten Freund anzeigt

Es ist November neunundneunzig
In der Universitätsbuchhandlung
Von Auburn / Alabama stehe ich lange
Vor den Regalen mit den Mappen
In Sandbraun und der Farbe Karmin

Den kleinen und großen Abreißblöcken
Für Komponisten denen hoch oben
Die paar Takte einfallen die
Sie nicht mehr vergessen dürfen
Während die Stewardeß die Fächer
Mit dem Daumenballen schließt

Den Notizbüchern in allen Größen
Dem *all weather notebook* mit
Seinem gelben Plastikdeckel
Für Wanderungen im Regen
Unter einem Schirm der
Den nördlichen Himmel zeigt
Oder für eine Fahrt im Ölzeug
Durch den Spray der Niagarafälle

Oder für dort wo es
Gar kein Wetter mehr gibt

Ich denke an mein erstes Schreibheft
Von meinem Großvater gemacht aus
Glänzendem dunkelroten Karton
Und ein paar Blättern Papier
Die er in der Mitte hineinnähte

Denke an einen Dichter aus Belgrad
Den ich in Lissabon traf und
Dem ich diesmal kein Notizbuch
Schenken werde sondern ein Gedicht

from *Brauchst du den Schlaf dieser Nacht*

In the hotel the waiters smile gently
I wrote in my notebook at breakfast
And strolling through the city
I bought myself an oversized address book
Sunflower-yellow with its index in Cyrillic
And because I did not want to spoil it
I did not enter a single name so that now
No name recalls a friend that has died

It is November nineteen-eighty-nine
In the university bookshop
Of Auburn / Alabama I stand for a long time
In front of the shelves of folders
Coloured sand brown and carmine

And the jotting pads large and small
For composers who over our heads
Dream up the perfect few bars which
They must not forget again
As the stewardess closes overhead lockers
With the ball of her thumb

The notebooks of all sizes
The all-weather notebook with
Its yellow plastic cover
For walks in the rain
Under an umbrella
Depicting the northern night-sky
Or for a trip in oilskins
Through the spray of the Niagara Falls

Or for the place
Where there is no more weather

I remember my first writing book
Made for me by my grandfather
It had shiny dark red cardboard
And a few sheets of paper
Which he had sewn in the middle

I remember a poet from Belgrade
Whom I met in Lisbon and whom
This time I won't be giving
A notebook but a poem

from *Do You Need This Night's Sleep*   57

In der Corner Bakery

Draußen war es November in Chicago
Leute mit offenem Kragen gingen vorbei
Und andere mit gepolsterten Mänteln
Alle trugen sie Sonnenbrillen unterwegs
In ein Land in dem es kalt war und
Ihnen die Sonne ins Gesicht schien

Über den dunklen Mantel einer Frau lief
Die vom Fenster gespiegelte Aufschrift
Raisin Pecan Flatbread Capucchino Mocha
So schnell daß man es nicht lesen konnte
Weil am Morgen die windige Stadt immer
Mit dem alten Spielzeug der Moderne spielt

Ich saß dort mehr als eine Stunde lang
In der Corner Bakery an der Erie Street
War mit allen Passanten fast verwandt
Und wenn ich mit der weißen Plastikgabel
Ein Stück Bacon and Eggs zum Mund führte
Schwebte meine Hand als Puppenhand hoch

Ich dachte an die Frau des Konsuls
Der Michelangelo und Puschkin übersetzt
Wir haben die Asche unseres Hundes
In der Urne aus Mailand hier in der Wohnung
Und keiner meiner Gedanken war schwerer
Als meine Hand oder die Handvoll Hund

from *Brauchst du den Schlaf dieser Nacht*

In the Corner Bakery

Outside it was November in Chicago
People walked by with open-necked shirts
Others with padded coats
All of them wearing sunglasses
In a country where it was cold and
The sun shone in their faces

The writing reflected from the shop-window
Ran across a woman's dark coat
Raisin Pecan Flatbread Capucchino Mocha
So fast you could hardly read it
Because in the morning the windy city always
Toys with the old playthings of modernity

I sat there for more than an hour
In the Corner Bakery on Erie Street
Felt almost related to all the passers-by
And each time I lifted a mouthful of bacon
And eggs to my mouth with the white plastic fork
My hand hovered in midair like the hand of a doll

I thought of the wife of the Consul
Who translated Michelangelo and Pushkin
We have the ashes of our dog
In the urn from Milan in our apartment
And none of my thoughts was heavier
Than my hand or the handful of dog

Die Teddybären

Der eine war ingwergelb
Er trug eine Lederhose
Wie viele Männer damals
Sein Fell hatte nie Haare gehabt
Große Poren die Haut eines Rauchers

Der andere war kleiner
Mit Strähnen braunen Haars
Am ganzen Körper
Dazwischen kahle Stellen ‚vom Krieg'
In dem er den Inhalt
Seines rechten Beins verloren hatte
Ich drückte den traurigen Stoff
Zwischen meinen Fingern

Sie sprachen kein Wort zueinander
Ich verstand daß der Raucher
Aus der Familie des Großvaters kam
Der Kriegsversehrte etwas
Von den Briefen wußte
Die der Bruder der Großmutter
Mit Bleistift nach Hause geschrieben hatte

Sie saßen und brüteten
Über ihren Geschichten
Die sie mir nicht erzählen wollten
Starrten auf ihre Beine und das leere Bein

An manchen Tagen waren sie Erwachsene
Die mich nicht ernstnahmen
Es war an einem Freitag oder es war
Abend oder es hatte seit Tagen geschneit

Oder es hatte seit Tagen geschneit
Und eine Schuld verschloß ihnen den Mund
Und wir hegten vielleicht denselben Verdacht
– daß es keinen Sinn haben würde
Meinen Vater der einem fremden Mann
Die abgerissene Hand wieder angenäht hatte
Um medizinischen Rat für das Bein zu fragen

from *Brauchst du den Schlaf dieser Nacht*

The Teddy Bears

One was the yellow of ginger
It wore leather britches
Like many men in those days
Its skin had never had fur
Huge pores the skin of a smoker

The other was smaller
With wisps of brown fur
All over his body
Bald patches where he'd been
'In the wars' and lost
The contents of his right leg
I pressed the miserable fabric
Between my fingers

They never spoke a word to each other
I gathered that the smoker
Came from my grandfather's family
The war veteran knew something
About the letters sent home
By my grandmother's brother
And written in pencil

They sat and brooded
Over their stories
Stories they did not want to tell me
Stared at their legs and the empty leg

Some days they were adults
Who would not take me seriously
It was a Friday or it was evening
Or it had been snowing for days

Or it had been snowing for days
And a guilty secret sealed their lips
And we harboured perhaps the same suspicion
– that it would make no sense
To ask my father who had sewed
The torn-off hand of a stranger back on
For medical advice about a leg

Sie lebten aber vielleicht hörten sie es schon
Nur auf sie gemünzt: *Nicht zu retten*
– wie der gefallene Bruder der Großmutter
Wie der leise zu mir redende rauchende Großvater
Der dafür bestraft worden war
Daß er – elegant wie ein Schauspieler
Auf dem violettfarbenen Kinoprogramm –
Unter dem Lichtschein der Stehlampe gesessen war
Zigarette zwischen den schlanken Fingern
Die eine Stelle in einem Buch liebkosten

They were alive but perhaps they heard
What seemed to be aimed at them: *beyond salvation*
Like my grandmother's fallen brother
Like my grandfather the smoker who spoke
Softly to me and was punished for the fact
That he – as elegant as one of the actors
On the violet-coloured cinema programme –
Had sat under the arc of the standard lamp
A cigarette between the slim fingers
That were caressing a paragraph in a book

Die Briefleserin

Sie steht im Profil beim Fenster
Von dem wir nur das Licht sehen
Blaue Jacke weißer Kragen langer Rock
Von ihrem aufgesteckten Haar
Fallen Locken über das Ohr
Als wollte sie nichts hören
Von dieser Welt
Als sei es ihr egal ob sie
Überrascht wird

Sie hält den Brief mit beiden Händen
Jedes Wort füllt ihr die Segel
Jedes einfache *schon* und
Der Montag und
Ein gelb-grauer Himmel und
Nächte ohne Schlaf

Lautlos singt sie den Brief
Von diesem Blatt
Singt jeden Satz auf dem Atem dessen
Der ihn schrieb

Sie steht ohne sich zu rühren im Licht
Während sie der süßen
Fremden Ordnung folgt
Überrascht und verführt
Verloren an den Willen in dieser Schrift

Auch wenn wir schwören
Ihr Komplize zu sein
Nur ihr Bild einatmen zu wollen
Müßten wir uns
Ohne ein Wort entschuldigen und
Schritt für Schritt von
Unserem Einbruch zurücknehmen

Sie sitzt vor ihrem Bildschirm
Aus dem ein Abendlicht auf sie strahlt
Die Nacht hält ihr Zimmer fest

from *Brauchst du den Schlaf dieser Nacht*

Woman Reading a Letter

She stands in profile at the window
From which we only see the light
Blue jacket white collar long frock
Curls fall over her ear
From her tied-up hair
As if she did not want to hear
Anything from this world
As if she did not care whether
She might be taken by surprise

She holds the letter in both hands
Each word fills her sails
Each simple *already* and
Monday and
A yellow-grey sky and
Nights without sleep

Without a sound she sight-reads
The song of the letter
Sings each sentence on the breath
Of the one who wrote it

She stands quite still in the light
All the time following
The sweet strange order
Surprised and seduced
Lost to the will in this writing

Even if we swear
That we are her accomplice
And only want to inhale her image
We would have to
Apologise without a word and
Retrace step by step
Our intrusion

She sits in front of the screen
With its dim light shining upon her
The night holds on tight to her room

Eine Hand hat sie aufgestützt
Mit dem Zeigefinger der anderen
Dirigiert sie den Computer
Läßt selbstvergessen und leicht
Die Zeilen in ihr Herz steigen

Ich wünsche mir einen Voyeur
Wie Vermeer so diskret
Der seine Scham mit ins Bild malt
Wenn er mir zusieht
Wie ich die Briefe lese
Jedes *wie war deine Nacht* und
Du klingst fröhlich sehr fin de siècle
Voriges fin de siècle natürlich
Und wie der Brief mich liest

Wie der Brief mich wieder
Und wieder liest
Sich nicht trennen kann
Von dem sich weitenden Schwarz
Meiner Pupillen
Bei der Stelle
Ich möchte so ehrlich sein wie du

Ich wünsche mir einen Voyeur
Der die Augen schließt
Wenn ich seine Schritte höre
Und schreibe *ich höre Schritte*
Und mit dem eiligen eiligen Druck
Meines Fingers den Brief und
Mich selbst verschwinden lasse

One hand propped up
The forefinger of the other
Conducts the computer
Lost to the world and lightly
Letting the lines rise into her heart

I would wish for a voyeur
As discreet as Vermeer
Who paints his shame into the picture
When he watches me
Reading the letters
Each *how was your night* and
You sound cheerful very fin de siècle
Last siècle of course
And the letter reading me

How the letter keeps reading me
Again and again
How it cannot let go
Of the widening black
In my pupils
At the passage
I want to be as honest as you are

I would wish for a voyeur
Who closes his eyes
When I hear his steps
And write *I hear steps*
And with a hasty hasty press
Of my finger make the letter
And myself disappear

Real Jardín Botánico

Am Allerseelentag passierte ich
Das metallene Drehkreuz und stand
Im Botanischen Garten in Madrid
Ockerfarbenes Laub lag überall und
Bewahrte das zu Ende gehende Licht auf

Die Rabatte waren zerzauste Gräber
Entlang der schmalen Alleen aufgereiht
Niedere Buxushecken faßten sie ein
Über die tags Kaninchen springen und
Die Pferdchen des Jenseits bei Nacht

Als einzige Pflanze blühte noch
Mexikanischer Salbei zwei Meter hoch
In seinem dunklen strahlenden Blau
Er bewegte sich zum Notgesang
Eines Polizeiwagens mit seinem Licht

Es gab einen Gemüsegarten mit Tomaten
Und man marschierte durch eine Laube
Aus dem gewundenen Holz des Weins
Es gab keine Bücher aber Rosenstöcke
Nach jungen Dichtern wie Keats benannt

Ich kam in einen Teil des Gartens
Dessen Herbst noch ungeübt aussah
Und ich wußte ich war ganz allein
Ich war gerade erst angekommen und
Das alles war für mich angelegt

from *Brauchst du den Schlaf dieser Nacht*

Real Jardín Botánico

On All Souls' Day I went through
The metal turnstile and stood
In the Botanical Garden in Madrid
Ochre leaves lay spread on the ground
And harboured the traces of the fading light

The border was fallen-down graves
Stood in rows along the narrow paths
Low box hedges enclosed them
Which rabbits jumped by day
And horses of the other world by night

The only plant still in bloom
Was a Mexican sage two metres tall
In its dark luminous blue
It swayed with the song of the siren
Of a police car with its light

There was a vegetable garden with tomatoes
And one passed through an arbour
Made from the twisted trunks of the vines
There were no books but rose trees
Named after young poets like Keats

I came into a part of the garden
Where autumn seemed not yet in practice
And I knew I was quite alone
I had only just arrived and
All this was laid out for me

Curriculum vitae

Zurückblickend sehe ich ein Reh
Wie es langen Anlauf nimmt und dort
Wo sich der Garten über den Zaun lehnt
Mühelos übersetzt wie es seine Schritte

Dem engeren Horizont anpaßt zu einem
Der Bäume geht sich aufrichtet und
Gierigen Fußes den Ast herunterbeugt
Wie ein Dieb wie es mit schrägem Blick

Dem Jäger das Versprechen abnimmt
Er werde sich bald von der Stelle
Rühren seine Flinte würde nicht
Zutraulich an seiner Wange und warm

Und das nächste war schon daß alles
So schnell ging wie jetzt wo die
Jahreszeiten sich kaum Zeit nehmen
Für mich so daß ich ihnen nachrufen muß

Und so als wollte ich es nochmal lernen
Mit betonter Langsamkeit lese und nicht
Wie man erwarten könnte geübter und
Mit Blick auf das was man weglassen kann

from *Brauchst du den Schlaf dieser Nacht*

Curriculum Vitae

Looking back I see how a deer
Takes a long run-up and at the place
Where the garden leans over the fence
Passes across with ease how it adjusts

Its pace to the narrow horizons goes
To one of the trees draws itself up and
Eagerly tramples the branch with its hoof
Like a thief how with a sideways glance

It takes the huntsman's word that
He will soon be gone from there that
His rifle will not be nestling
Trusty against his cheek and warm

And the next thing was that it all
Went so quickly just like now when
The seasons scarcely make time enough
For me so that I must call after them

And as if I wanted to learn it again
I read haltingly slowly and not
As one might expect with more polish
And an eye for what to leave out

from *Do You Need This Night's Sleep* 71

aus

Das Talent meiner Frau

from

My Wife's Talent

Das Talent meiner Frau

Wie sollte ich wissen daß sie
als Füchsin über das Buch eines
Fremden schritt Nase hochgereckt in
den Dezembersturm Augen geschlossen
gegen den weißtanzenden Wind das
weiße Fell auf der Brust gescheitelt
zu einem dunklen Strich Hinterbeine
fast versunken wie sollte ich wissen
daß sie in Schatten von Buchstaben
trat schwarze Gene unter Midwestschnee

My Wife's Talent

How was I to know that she was walking
As a vixen across a stranger's book
Her nose stretched high into the
December storm her eyes closed
Against the white dancing wind the
White fur on her chest parted
To a dark line hind-legs
Almost sunk how was I to know
That she was stepping into shadows of
Letters black genes under Midwest snow

Anvertraut

In fremden Tagen würde ich stehn
mit selber Gebärde Stirn und
Gestirn mit einem Strich Sahara
zurückkommen vom Fensterbrett

So wenig kannst du je von mir
wissen als gehörte ich heimlich
einem andern Glauben an feierte
mit dem Rücken zu dir Jahrtausend

Am Bahnhof wollten wir uns treffen
im Café auf dem Weg sah ich dich
draußen mit großen Schritten
vorbeieilen zu mir

Entrusted

In stranger days I would be standing
With the selfsame gesture brow and
Star sign would be coming back from
The windowsill with a film of Sahara dust

You can know so little about me
As if I had secretly joined
Another creed celebrated
A millennium with my back to you

At the station we wanted to meet
In the café on the way I saw you
Hurrying past with large strides
Towards me

Ilse

Wenn ich losließe
würde mich dein Karussell weit
hinausschleudern dein später Ruf
fiele schon in einen fremden Schoß

aus *Das Talent meiner Frau*

Ilse

If I just let go at once
Your carousel would fling
Me off your late call would
Fall into some stranger's lap

Flitterjahre

Wir spüren die Widerrede
vor dem linken Fenster schneit es
dichter als vor dem rechten wir sind
Wissende die sich neu ins Alte verlieben
vernarrt in den Umriß ihrer Wünsche *komm*
laß uns einen Hund holen wir laufen ihm
nach bis ins fremde Gebell bis in
die Wahrsagung meiner Innenhand

aus *Das Talent meiner Frau*

Honeymoon Years

We sense the contradiction
The snow seems heavier out of
The window on the left than the right
We are initiates falling in love all over again
With what they already know infatuated
With the shape of their desires *come*
Let's get ourselves a dog we'll follow him
Into the strange barking chase him into
The fortune read in my palm

Mystifikation

Wovon hast du mich soeben befreit? von
den Stimmen im Garten die die Leiter
hinauf steigen von letzten Astern
in acht Farben zwei Finger zuviel
ich kann den Abschied nicht gestatten
du gehst als würdest du gerade kommen
auf jedem Blau das man für Laub mißliest

aus *Das Talent meiner Frau*

Mystification

What have you just released me from?
The voices in the garden that come creeping
Up the ladder the last asters of autumn
In eight different colours two fingers too many
I can't allow you to leave like this you are
Going as if you were just arriving with
Every shade of blue that one misreads for true

Madame B. plädiert

Ich lag vergiß das nicht
mit Stirn und Nasenrücken
in der Beuge seines Arms
ich lag die fellnasse Beute
und streunte nachhaus also
stell mir ein Bein binde
die Füße *mir bring ihn*
zum Stillstand unruhig
seufzenden Schritt zur Tür

aus *Das Talent meiner Frau*

Madame B. Pleads

I was lying don't forget
With my forehead the bridge
Of my nose in the crook of his arm
I was lying a sodden prey
I was wandering home so
Trip me up and bind my feet
But *bring me* some peace
From this sighing this restless
Pacing to the door for *him*

Brandywine Valley

Ich stehe in der Scheune
an die zerkratzte blaue Tür
gelehnt Licht fällt scharf
in einen Eimer ich trage
es über Stufen aus Holz
die ich nur rückwärts
hinuntergehen kann Heuboden
Winterhafen ich leere es ins
trockene Boot zieh die Schuhe
aus lege meinen Kopf an den
gestreiften Matrosensack
mit den Schätzen des Hundes

aus *Das Talent meiner Frau*

Brandywine Valley

I am standing in the barn
Leaning against the scratched
Blue door light falls sharply
Into a bucket I carry it
Up the wooden steps
Which I can only go down
Backwards hayloft
Winter harbour I empty it
Into the dry boat take off
My shoes lay my head on
The striped sailor's kitbag
With the dog's treasures

Lektion

Was ich gelernt habe
wollte ich aufzählen
wie ich einen kühlen Namen
in der Hand halte wenn ich
die Klinke drücke wie
ich das Wegschild verkehre
die Fische mit dem Kopf
am Stein totschlage
der Dreh ist mir schon
so vertraut und wie ich
während die Kiemenblutspritzer
trocknen vom roten ins schwarze
Kleid wechsle

da legte mir der Kater
der auf meinem Schoß saß
die Pfote auf das Handgelenk
und ich wußte nicht ob
zur Beruhigung oder weil er
so an den toten Fisch glaubte

aus *Das Talent meiner Frau*

Lesson

I wanted to list
What I have learned
How I hold a cool
Name in my hand when
I touch the doorknob how
I turn the road sign around
Kill the fish by striking
Their heads on the stone
I have practised till I have
The knack and how I change
Dresses while the splashes of
Gill-blood are drying
From red to black

The cat which was sitting
On my lap laid his paw
On the back of my hand
And I did not know whether
It was to calm me or because
He so believed in the dead fish

Der Sarkophag des Ehepaars im Museo Etrusco, Villa Giulia, Rom

Sie liegt den Oberkörper aufgerichtet
auf ihren linken Arm gestützt er liegt
in gleicher Stellung hinter ihr ein
wenig höher auf dem Kissen seine Hand
Gewicht das sie im Wachsein nie verschob
liegt so auf ihrer Schulter daß sein
Daumenballen die Höhle ihres Nackens
streicheln kann wie sie es immer liebte
wie sie es auch dem Kater tat

Mit ausgestrecktem Finger seiner leichten
Hand erklärt er ihr die Gipfelnamen
dieser Ewigkeit das also bleibt
denkt sie sein Orientierungssinn
und wie daheim die Hügel unsrer
Tolfaberge und die Monti Sabatini
werd ich auch diese hier verwechseln
und –– das Boot der erste Anblick
dieses Boots ein ganz normales
Fischerboot wo Bug und Heck bemalt
sind doch womit das wollte sie nicht
sehen es bedeutete vielleicht auch gar
nichts weil dies Zeichenlesen nun zu
Ende war ––

Sie denkt an ihre Freunde mit denen
sie so viele Schalen leerten die ihre
Lieblingskissen hatten so wie sie
sich beim Bankett bei ihnen immer
wie zuhause fühlten die beiden Männer
nie den Skorpion im andern reizten und
sie würde ihnen gern jetzt sagen daß
man nicht in einem Pferdewagen ankommt

aus *Das Talent meiner Frau*

The Married Couple's Sarcophagus in the Museo Etrusco, Villa Giulia, Rome

She is lying with her upper body raised
And rests her weight on her left arm he is
Lying in the same position behind her
A little higher on the cushion his hand
A weight she would never brush away
When awake rests on her shoulder so that
With the ball of his thumb he can stroke the
Hollow of her throat just the way she'd always
Loved and as she had also done to the cat

One finger of his light hand stretched out
He shows her the names of the mountains
In this eternity so this is still there she thinks
His sense of direction and just as
At home I confused the hills of our
Tolfa Mountains and the Monti Sabatini
I shall confuse these ones here
And –– the boat the first sight of
That boat an ordinary fishing boat
With a painted bow and stern but
What was painted on it she did not
Want to know and maybe it was all
The same because this reading of the signs
Had ceased ––

She is thinking of their friends with whom
They emptied many bowls together who had their
Favourite cushions just as they themselves
Felt quite at home at their friends'
Banquets as neither of the men would
Tease the scorpion in the other and
She would be happy now to tell them
One does not arrive in horse-drawn chariots

Jener Abend als der Freund vom Totenhaus
zu sprechen anfing wie er die Wände sich
bemalen lassen will mit Jagdglück einem
Zelt in dem die Beute von der Decke hängt
mit Leoparden die auf weichen Pfoten
patrouillieren Tänzerinnen ihren Fuß
erhoben so daß man den Tanzschritt
weiterdenkt und du – er griff nach unten
zu dem Hund der immer mit zu Gast war –
wirst auch aufgemalt und überhaupt wir
alle wie wir sind und wie wir bleiben

Den will ich sehen fuhr er fort der
uns die Tische leert die Vasen
wegschleppt von den Wänden wie schon
vorkam daß man Waffen raubte Werkzeug
Trinkgefäße Statuetten oder denkt ihr
sollte man wie's manche tun die Betten
Stühle in den Tuff der Kammer schneiden?

Es war der Abend als zum erstenmal
der Grieche da war dessen Rat Geschmack
und Urteil sich der Gatte später anvertraute
sie aber las das eingelernte Wissen über
fremde Bräuche vom Gesicht ihm ab die Frau
beim Gastmahl dieses *Gattin nicht Hetäre*
war in seinen Blick geschrieben machte
ihr den Abend kurz –– das Boot das
Boot war Boden der mit Wasser spielte
Nötigung zu einem langen Schritt ––

Der Grieche ging im Haus herum ließ sich
vom Gatten die Amphoren zeigen Meisterstücke
eines Freundes der gereist war und den
Stil aus Ionien wie kein anderer
beherrschte aber machtlos war wie alle
wenn ein Vogel eine Lebensstraße quert
die Werkstatt seither leer kein Herakles
vollbringt mehr eine Tat auf seinem Ton

That evening when their friend began to talk
About the House of the Dead how he would
Have walls painted with the scenes of a successful
Hunt a tent where prey hangs from the ceiling
And with leopards patrolling on soft paws
Dancing girls with one foot raised so one
Imagines step for step and follows the dance
And you – he reached down to the dog
That came with them each visit – you will
Be painted here as well and all of us
As we are here and as we shall remain

I'd like to see the man he then continued who
Could clear our tables steal the vases
From the walls as has already happened
Weapons robbed and tools and
Drinking vessels statuettes or do you
Think we should have our beds and chairs
Cut in the chamber's tufa as others do?

That evening was the first time that the Greek
Was there in whose advice good taste and
Judgement her dear husband later put his faith
She however read all his knowledge
About foreign customs in his face the woman
At the banquet this *wife not a hetaira*
Was written in his eyes it whiled away
The evening for her –– the boat the
Boat was ground that played with water
The necessity of such a step ––

The Greek was wandering round the house
He had her husband show him the amphorae
Masterpieces by a friend who had been travelling
Had mastered the Ionic style like no one else
But he was helpless just like everybody is
When the bird is crossing your life's path
And ever since his workshop has been empty
No Hercules completes a labour on his clay

Der Grieche zog ein feines Lächeln auf
als man den Namen nannte und sie hätte
gern gehört wie er aus seinem Munde
klang ob man den Helden hier entkräfte
weil man vielleicht die Zunge anders an
den Gaumen tippe doch der junge Gast
erzählte schon von einem Meister dessen
Vasen alles überträfen Exekias aus Athen
ein Töpfer Maler Seelenfänger der
die sagenhaften Kämpfer wie von weitem
unbeobachtet jedoch zugleich aus aller
nächster Nähe ganz genau studiere und
den Augenblick erwarte da sie
unverwechselbar sich zeigen

Es gebe eine Vase um die man wie um
Helena Krieg führen könnte so – der
Grieche schloß die Augen weil das Bild
der Vase nur in ihm war und beschrieb
was er da sah – Achill und Ajax sitzen bei
dem Würfelspiel die Körper vorgelehnt
so daß der halbe Hocker freibleibt und
die Köpfe konzentriert hinabgebeugt
die Waffen hinten an die Wand gelehnt
die auch die Wand des Kruges ist
einzig die Speere halten sie in ihrer
linken Hand bei Ajax sieht es aus als
kraule er sich mit dem Speer den Bart

Der Gatte sah sie an und während
er den Blick nicht von ihr ließ
erzählte er dem Griechen daß sie
solches angespannte Warten in der
Mitte des Amphorenbauchs nicht schätze
zwei Kämpfer jeder in des andren Blick
gesperrt zwei Monsterhunde mit tropfenden
Zungen wartend auf das Zeichen in der
Pupille des anderen die Gattin sagte er

aus *Das Talent meiner Frau*

The Greek just smiled a gentle smile on
Hearing that name spoken and yes she would
Have liked to hear how he pronounced it
Whether perhaps the hero was weakened here
Because the tip of their tongue touches
Their palate in a different way but the young guest
Was already telling them about a master
Whose vases were the best there were in Athens
A potter painter catcher of souls who
Studied legendary warriors from a distance
Unobserved but at the same time from
So very close and waited for
The moment when they would
At last reveal themselves

There was a vase he said for whose sake one might
Wage a war just like they did for Helen – the
Greek youth closed his eyes because the image
Of the vase was in his mind and he described
What he was seeing – Achilles and Ajax sitting
Playing at a game of dice their bodies leaning
Forward so they are half risen from their stools
Their heads bowed down in concentration
Their weapons stacked against the wall behind
Which is also the inside of the vase
Except their spears which they hold in
Their hands and Ajax looks as if
He is combing it right through his beard

The husband looked at her and while he
Held her gaze with his
He told the Greek she did not much
Appreciate such tension in the
Middle of the vase's belly
Two warriors whose eyes are locked
Two monstrous dogs with lolling
Tongues and waiting for the tiniest sign
In the opponent's pupil now my wife he said

und drehte sich dem Gast zu zieht Motive
vor die rund um die Amphoren laufen halb
ernste Jagden die jeden Augenblick in Tanz
umspringen können schlanke weiße Hunde
die einander beinah überholen die als
gemalte Fabelwesen spüren daß man auf
der Töpferscheibe schon als sie noch gar
nicht existierten sie ins Rennen sandte
Schicksal das sich übertrug aus Händen
die ganz andres taten – und er lachte

Es wird die Mode jetzt in Attika begann
der Gast daß man nicht nur die Schönheit
eines Jünglings lobt mit einem Spruch am
Rand der Vase *ho pais kalos* ich sah auch
schon die schöne junge Frau gepriesen
(Gattin nicht – Hetäre dachte sie)
– – ein Schritt und was wenn man das Boot
verfehlt? verfehlt man dann das Jenseits?
gibt es mehrere davon? ist dieser falsche
Schritt ein zweites Sterben quer zum Tod – –

Der Gatte hielt den jungen Mann beim
Arm und unter ungezählten scharfen
Steinen wie aus einer Schleuder direkt
auf die Wände ihres Herzens hörte sie ihm
zu wie er den Sarkophag beschrieb den er
für sich und seine Gattin bilden lassen
wollte fremd so fremd war er mit diesen
Einzelheiten – ohne sie doch für sie
beide ausgedacht der Grieche stand in
Fesseln so als redete ein bisher
unbekannter Gott zu ihm

Wie schnell ihm dann der Plan des Gatten
in die Hände sprang er zählte ihre Zöpfe
nahm jeden in die Hand und legte ihn zurück
auf ihren Nacken je zwei nach vorn je einen
links und rechts der unter ihrem Ohr
entspringt die Schulter rund hinunter
daß sie kaum zu atmen wagte weil doch
alles unverrückbar werden sollte

aus *Das Talent meiner Frau*

And turned to the young guest prefers such
Motifs as run around outside of the amphorae
Pursuits half in earnest that may break into a
Dance at any moment slender white dogs
Which almost catch each other up and which
As painted creatures of fable know that
On the potter's wheel before they even
Came into their being they were sent off
Into a race a fate passed on from hands
Busy with something else – he laughed

There is a fashion now in Athens said the guest
That dedications on the vase's rim
Need not just praise the beauty of a boy
Alone *ho pais kalos* I have also seen
A beautiful young woman praised
(Not wife – hetaira she was thinking)
–– one step and what if with one missing step
You miss the boat? And miss the next world then?
Or is there more than one? Does this one false
Step bring a second end in spite of death ––

The husband held the young man's arm
And as if a sling had sent innumerable
Sharp stones raining down onto her
Heart's walls she listened to him how he
Described the sarcophagus that he wanted
To have built for himself and his wife
And strange he was so strange with all
Those details – conceived without her but
For both of them the Greek was standing
Rooted to the spot as if a god so far
Unknown to everybody was addressing him

How fast the husband's plan leaped straight
Into his hands he counted out her plaits
Took each in turn into his hands and set it back
In place two down the front those
On the left and right behind her ears
He laid over her shoulders so that
She scarcely dared breathe in since
Everything would now be set in stone

from *My Wife's Talent*

Die Augen sollten sein wie Mandeln in
den Winkeln außen weit hinaufgezogen
und die Kappe für das Haar muß glatt
sein hoch ansetzen und der Bart des
Gatten spitz er sprach mit solcher
Festigkeit als könnte er die Blitze
mit der flachen Hand vertreiben und
sie wußte nicht ob sich die Götter
das gefallen lassen und –– das Boot
war Nacht am Kleidersaum war Greifen
nach der Hand des Gatten ––

Lange Wochen drehte sie den Kopf zur
Seite wenn der Gatte bei den Zeichnungen
der Künstler auf dem Boden kniete wollte
nicht ans Wasser keine Rufe hören her von
andren Ufern nicht mehr in den Spiegel
blicken der ihr Bild verkleinert ihre
Ringe saßen lose und sie ließ den Hasen
fallen schönstes Ölgefäß ein Ohr brach ab

Daß die Dinge auch ein zweites Leben
haben daß sie auch das Wasser überqueren
daß sie unversehrt dort hingelangen daß
an dieser Decke diesem Kissen hier die
nachgebildet sind und hart wie wir auch
nachgebildet sind und hart nur keiner
Schaden tut und eine Ecke abschlägt ach
er wüßte nicht daß unser Hund so gern
am Kissenzipfel kaute

Sie denkt zurück an eine andre Nacht
als sie die Handbewegungen der Tänzerin
nachzeichnete in diese stille Luft in
ihrem Schlafgemach zwei Mittelfinger
eingeschlagen die andern Finger weg
gespreizt das Drehen in dem Handgelenk
das sagte *du mußt schneller sein wenn du*
und was das traute sie sich nie zu fragen

aus *Das Talent meiner Frau*

The eyes should be like almonds drawn
Out far beyond the outside corners
the cap then for her hair should be
Quite smooth on her high forehead and the
Husband's beard be pointed thus he spoke
With certainty as if he could turn lightning
Away with the flat of his hand
She did not know whether the gods
Were willing to allow this and –– the boat
Was night along the hem of her long gown
Was reaching for her husband's hand ––

For weeks she turned her head away
Each time her husband knelt down with the
Artist's sketches spread out on the floor
She did not want to see the water nor to hear
The calling from the other shores nor look
Into the mirror which reduced her image
Her rings were loose she dropped the rabbit
Her finest oil jar and an ear broke off

That objects too should have another
Life that they should also cross the water
That they should get there in one piece that
No one should do damage to this blanket
This cushion which are sculpted and are
Hard as we are also sculpted and are hard
No one should break a corner off but then
He could not know how much our dog loved
Chewing at the corner of the cushion

She thinks back to a different night
When she was sketching movements
Of the dancer's hands into her bedroom's
Quiet air two middle fingers were
Turned in her other fingers were
Splayed back and when she turned her wrist
It said *you have to be much quicker if you*
But she never dared ask what

Das Boot war wirklich Boot und mehr als
Boot wie überhaupt so vieles wie im Leben
ist und dennoch anders hier *begrüßt* man
eine Farbe mit dem ganzen Wesen fast
Gebet es gibt die rote Erde immer noch das
Schwarz der Helden auf den Vasen das
Versteckspiel dunkelgrüner Bäume und – –
das Boot war Boden der mit Wasser spielte
Nötigung zu einem langen Schritt war
Nacht am Kleidersaum war Greifen nach
der Hand des Gatten war das Wissen daß
der Tod sie beide holte höchstes Glück

Mit ausgestrecktem Finger seiner
leichten Hand zeigt er auf uns
die sich im Leben noch spazierend
ihnen nähern solche waren wir sagt er
so gingen wir herum und fanden
unsere liebsten Plätze suchten nach
den Stücken die uns fehlen für das
Glück der Augen auch die toten Augen sehen

The boat was really boat and more
Than boat as everything is as in life
And yet so different here you *welcome*
Any colour with your whole being almost
A prayer there is still the red soil the
Black of the heroes on the vases the
Hide-and-seek of dark green trees and --
The boat was ground that played with
Water necessity of such a step was night
Along the hem of her long gown was reaching for
Her husband's hand was knowing that death
Would come for both of them that utter bliss

One finger of his light hand
Is stretched out he points at us
Still walking our path through life
But drawing near to them now such were we
He says this was how we found
Our dearest places looking
For the things we lacked for
Our eyes' happiness even dead eyes see

Fischblut

Alle Flüsse hinauf wäre ich ihm
gefolgt wie es im Märchen heißt so
zog er mich in seinen Strom immer
genau die fünf Töne voraus die ich
mir in den Kopf gesetzt hatte und
kaum lag ich auf seinem nassen Brett
sagte eine Stimme wenn die Sonne
in den Räucherofen fällt glitzern
die Brassen wie Barren Golds

Fish Blood

I would have swum up any river
For his sake just like the fairytales
That is how he caught me in his wake
Always five notes ahead the very five
That I had taken into my head
And scarcely was I lying on his wet board
When a voice said if the sunlight
Falls into the smokehouse the
Braces glitter like ingots of gold

Was sie ihrem Eroberer Sir Francis auftrug

Wenn du ins Treibeis gerätst sammle
die untreuen Versprechen ein bring mir
alle unter deren Namen ich meine
Unterschrift gesetzt guten Glaubens
bring was sie mir in die Zöpfe flochten
was meinen Kopf beschwert lebenslang und
vom beleuchteten Ende der Welt bring mir
das Aufflackern seines nein irgend
eines Pulses und töte den Drachen bring
mir sein Wort zurück das du mir gabst und
brich dir kein Fersenbein beim Sprung an Land

aus *Das Talent meiner Frau*

What Instructions She Gave Her Conqueror
Sir Francis

When you get into drift-ice collect
The unfaithful promises bring me
All those under whose names I put
My signature in good faith
Bring what they braided into my plaits
Which will weigh me down as long as I live and
From the illuminated ends of the earth bring me
The flicker of his – no – of anyone's
Pulse and slay the dragon bring
Back his word that you gave me and
Don't crack your heel when jumping ashore

Die Vier Hilliards

Ein grünes ein blaues ein gelbes
ein rotes Hemd ein grünes ein gelbes
ein blaues ein rotes Hemd ein Hemd
ein Hemd ein Hemd ein Hemd ein grünes
kein blaues ein gelbes kein rotes ein
Hemd ein grünblaues rotgelbes Hemd und
noch lange nachdem sie gelandet schwingen
die Trapeze schwenken Weihrauch in den
Kirchenraum

aus *Das Talent meiner Frau*

The Four Hilliards

A green a blue a yellow
A red shirt a green a yellow
A blue a red shirt a shirt
A shirt a shirt a shirt a green one
Not blue a yellow one not red a
Shirt a greenblue redyellow shirt and
For a long time after they have landed
The trapezes are swinging incense into
This vast church

Auf ein Foto Iosif Brodskijs

beim Begräbnis von Anna Achmatova

Du bist ein Mann im Wintermantel
Kragen und der Schal stehn ab
wo du herkommst aus dem Dorf mit vierzehn
Hütten Kandidat für Blechgesang und Wind
kann dich Frost im Nacken nicht erschüttern

Aber ihr Gesicht ein weicher Stein
wie von zwei Händen hingelegt läßt zu
daß alles kippt die Hierarchie der Zweige
Stufen zur Veranda Rußlands Wale
unter dem Planeten sind verrückt

Ihr Profil die unverwechselbare
Narbe ihres Landes zieht dich mit
du wehrst dich gegen diesen Sog
bedeckst dir Mund und Kinn
die Wange mit gespreizter Hand

Man stellt sich vor du weinst
dein Mund (den du beschreiben wirst
als schreckliche Ruine) zuckt du weißt
vermutlich nicht wie schön er ist
wie unzerstörbar richtig seine Linien

Hinter deine vorgehaltne Hand
fällt der gezählte Blick der Sprache
--- --- --- --- --- --- ---
Niemand flüstert sie *wird*
meinem Wunsch so sehr entsprechen

Nacht für Nacht wirst du zu ihr gehen
unter deinem fremden Namen dann
in blauem Leinen ewig in Angst sie
zu verlieren weil eine andere
in dein geöffnetes Herz starrt

On a Photograph of Joseph Brodsky

at the funeral of Anna Akhmatova

You are a man in a winter coat
Your collar and scarf stand out
Where you come from a village with just
Fourteen huts candidate for brass music and wind
Frost in the neck cannot shake you

Her face a stone but soft as if
Two hands had laid it there
Allows the hierarchy of twigs to tilt
Stairs up to the veranda Russia's whales
Under the planet are out of kilter

Her profile the unmistakable
Scar of her country draws you in
You fight against this undertow
Cover your mouth and chin
And cheek with outstretched hand

One might imagine you are weeping
Your mouth (which you will describe
As a horrible ruin) twitches you probably
Don't know how beautiful it is
How indestructibly exact its lines

Behind the hand held up to your mouth
The numbered glances of language falling
--- --- --- --- --- --- ---
No one it whispers *will*
Meet my desires like you

Night after night you will go to her
Under your foreign name then
In blue linen always afraid of
Losing her because another woman
Is staring into your opened heart

Birdwatching

für R.S. Thomas

Der alte Dichter saß neben mir der
beim Umblättern so zitterte die Seiten
schlug mit der flachen Hand morgen sagte er
fliege er an die polnisch-russische Grenze
Vögel studieren im Freien ich sah Ikarus
stürzen durch sein zuckendes Fernglas
nach jedem Gedicht ein Blick auf die Uhr

aus *Das Talent meiner Frau*

Birdwatching

For R.S. Thomas

The old poet was sitting beside me who
Trembled so much as he turned the pages hitting
Each one with the flat of his hand the following day
He said he was flying to the Polish–Russian border
A spot of birdwatching out of doors I saw Icarus
Fall through his twitching binoculars
After each poem a glance at his watch

Schuhe zählen

Schwarze Turnschuhe für die Jungen
rote für Mädchen über dem Rist
zwei Stretchgummifinger

Vier Reihen schwarzer Schuhe mit
drin ausgespanntem Holzfuß die
Schuhwand des Dichters Bernhard

Dreitausend Paar in seidenen Farben
oder sind es mehr aus denen
Donna Imelda die Wahl treffen
muß für ihre brennenden Sohlen

Drei Paar Stiefel auf einem Polizeitisch
aufgereiht wie Vater Mutter und Sohn was
ist die kleinste Größe mit Stahlkappen
im Geschäft und dann in einer Junisamstagnacht
als sie seinen Kopf mit Füßen traten

Adolf Eichmann in seiner Zelle auf der
Matratzenpritsche liegend Buch in der Hand
dunkle Socken die Kontur seines Überbeins
auf dem Boden ein Paar Großmutterhausschuhe
mit Fellkragen den man hochklappen kann

Viele graue Slipper aus Zwirn hinter
einer Glaswand im Holocaust Museum

aus *Das Talent meiner Frau*

Counting Shoes

Black plimsolls for the boys
Red for the girls and over the instep
Two fingers of stretchy rubber

Four rows of black shoes with
The wooden shoe-tree open inside the
Shoe rack of Bernhard the writer

Three thousand silk pairs in all the colours
Of the rainbow or is it more that
Donna Imelda has to choose from
To house her burning soles

Three pairs of boots on a police table
In a row like father mother son what
Is the smallest size in the shop with steel
Toecaps and then on a Saturday night in
June as they are kicking his head in

Adolf Eichmann in his cell lying on
His mattress bed a book in his hand
Dark socks the contour of his ganglion
On the floor a pair of grandma's house-shoes
With a collar of fur to pull up round his ankle

Countless grey slippers made of thread in
A glass case in the Holocaust Museum

Dritte Bombennacht

Mit einer Stimme so sanft
als hauche sie ihrem Kind
die letzten störenden Bilder
vor dem Schlaf weg sagte
CNN's Christiane Amanpour
live aus Bagdad, *uuuuuh,*
wwwow, that was a big one.

Third Night of Bombing

In a voice as gentle
As if she were blowing away
The last troubling images
Before her child sleeps
CNN's Christiane Amanpour said
Live from Baghdad, *uuuuuh,*
Wwwow, that was a big one.

aus
Der Schnabelberg

from
The Schnabelberg

Nachruf

Früher mußte ich manchmal die
Freude verscheuchen war so froh
und lebendig vor dem Schlaf früher
sank ich mit meinem ersten Gedanken
an dich sanfter Fallschirm in den
Tag diese schwere unheilbare Liebe
sagst du hat sie nun hinter sich

Obituary

Once there were times when I had to
Chase away my happiness was so happy
So alive when it was time to sleep
Once I would float down into
The day on my first thought
Of you gentle parachute the worst
Of this severe and incurable love
Is behind her now you say

Kalte Aprilnacht

Sie sagen heute nacht steht Frost
ums Haus du machst ein Feuer unterm
Kirschbaum so bewacht von deiner Glut
möcht ich auch blühen klirren halb
verbrennen retten meine weiße Zeit

Cold April Night

They say tonight there will be a frost
At the house you lay a fire under
The cherry tree watched over by your heat
Like that I'd like to blossom whither
Half burn away salvage my white time

Neues Lied

Heut hab ich mich wieder singen
gehört ich untreue Amsel auf der
Antenne es sei also ein Baum auch
wenn mir die Krallen zittern

aus *Der Schnabelberg*

New Song

Today I caught myself singing again
An unfaithful blackbird on the
Aerial which will have to be my tree
Even if my claws are trembling

Concierge

Ich trau meiner Ruhe nicht
immer wieder schlägst du in
meinen kühlen Zimmern alles kurz
und klein weil sie die Arme weit
auftut und sagt hier ist Platz

aus *Der Schnabelberg*

Concierge

I don't trust my peace and quiet
Time and again you smash
Everything in my cool rooms
To pieces because it opens
Its arms says here is space for you

Schönes Versäumnis

Ich müßte jetzt auch nicht fragen
hab ich den See seinen kühlen
nächtlichen Traum der meine Seele
beschlug hab ich den See an dessen
Saum ich mich erstmals an dich
geschmiegt wieder ausgeweint?

aus *Der Schnabelberg*

A Fine Omission

And now of course I shouldn't
Go and ask: the lake with its cool
Night-time dreams which misted up
My soul the lake on the shores
Of which we first lay side by side
Have I cried it out again?

Dressurakt

Ich hab meine Sehnsucht gezähmt
du kannst sie besuchen bürsten
gegen den Strich schöner sich
gleich legender Widerstand sie
scharrt sie frißt dir aus der
hohlen Hand sie geht wenn du ihr
einen Namen gibst mit dir durch

aus *Der Schnabelberg*

Dressage

I have tamed my longing
You can visit rub it up
The wrong way feel the
Brief resistance it will paw
The ground eat right out of
Your hand and if you give
It a name it will go the distance

Modus barbaricus

Wenn ich aus allen Bäumen dich
gejagt die Gräser ausgekehrt die
Vögel ziehn hab lassen schnabelleer
wenn auch die stumme Nacht nicht mehr
von dir nur schweigt und doch sich
alles nachfüllt bleibt nur dies:
ich wird dich ohne mich nicht los

Modus Barbaricus

Once I have chased you from each and
Every tree swept out the grass and let
The birds depart with empty beaks
And even the silent night keeps
Secrets apart from you just to see it all
Fill up again there's only one thing for it:
I can't be rid of you and not be rid of me

aus *Versuchungen*

IX

In deiner Augen Hochmoor braune Tiefe
Ruht ein Blick den du nicht weitergibst.
Als ob die ungeborne Zukunft schliefe
Kind wie du nie die Lider hebst.
Wir haben nichts das weich und klein
Vor unsern Knien steht sind Eltern nur
Für uns. Durchs Zwischenland führt fein
Was wir uns ohne Umweg tun verborgne Spur.
Ich leb in stillen Zimmern gut mit dir
Auf Reisen. Bücherherz das Sprünge macht.
Du fragst fragst nicht. Du liegst bei mir.
Wir atmen Träume voneinander jede Nacht.
Dann schieben unsre wachen Seelen schwer
Kulissen fremdvertraute hin und her.

XI

Manchmal legst du dich der Sonne in
Den Weg als müßtest Gras Gras Erde Gras
Du aus mir machen nimmst dir wildes Maß
Drückst meine Weichen die Betrügerin.
So eng auf mir. So weit zu dir. Es ruft
Dein Herzschlag links weiß daß die Welt
Sich dreht auf deinem Weg zu mir verfehlt
Mich um kein Gramm. Dein süßer Atemduft.
Ich sage: Wolltest Schnee du werden
Ließe ich mich auch herab ich spielte dir
Damit du deckend liegenbliebst auf mir
Die kalte strenge totgestellte Erde.
Würde alles spüren. Senken Mulden
Wimpern Wald auch würde alles dulden.

aus *Der Schnabelberg*

from *Temptations*

IX

You won't pass on the person that you keep
Buried in the moors of your brown eyes.
As if the unborn future lay asleep
The image of a child that will not rise.
We have no one before us tiny and forlorn
Are parents only to ourselves so we
Can watch the empty space between us form
The hidden pathways of our destiny.
We rest in quiet rooms. My bookish heart
May skip a beat but isn't what it seems.
You ask you don't. We lie a skin apart.
At night we breathe each other's dreams.
But then our souls awake and intervene
Strange and familiar change the scene.

XI

Sometimes you lie so you block out the sun
As if you wanted me to turn from grass
Into bare earth you size me up and down
You force my flesh. I'm your adulteress.
So close to me. So far from you. I hear
Your heartbeat calling me it knows the earth
Is turning as I sense you drawing near
And meeting me. The sweet smell of your breath.
I say that if you wanted to be snow
I would lie down and play my part and be
The winter earth turned cold and hard so
You could be a blanket over me.
I would feel everything; however small
Curves hollows lashes trees. I'd take it all.

Handwerkszeug

Am Ledermesser des Großvaters
klebt nur blutheller Rost
die gekrümmte wie türkische Klinge
pflügte auf seinen Bauch zu
schnitt Treibriemen Schuhsohlen aus

Nikotin der harte Glanz des Eherings
stumm nahm der Holzgriff
die fremde Maserung für gegeben

Ich weiß nicht mehr wie roch
dieser große Mann dessen Blick
sich zu mir gebeugt frühweißes Haar
noch ehe er so alt war wie ich jetzt
Es blieb: wie er ein flatterndes faustgroßes
Herz in den Käfig meiner Hand gelockt
mir die Finger um den Bleistift
schloß und sagte Schreib!

aus *Der Schnabelberg*

Tools of the Trade

Only a smear of blood-bright rust
Stains my grandfather's leather-cutter
The curved almost Turkish blade
Would slice towards his stomach
Cutting out drive-belts and leather soles

Nicotine the hard glint of his wedding ring
Silently the wooden handle took
The strange grain as given

I no longer remember the smell
Of this huge man whose face
Bent down to mine hair prematurely white
Before he was as old as I am now
What remains is how he lured a fluttering
Heart as big as a fist into the cage
Of my hand closed my fingers
Round the pencil and said *Write*

Zehnjähriger

Dieser nicht trocknende Stumpf so
bunt der Krieg wie Rosen im Schnee
für immer führt dich deine Kindheit
an der Hand die du verlorst

Ten Years Old

This stump that does not heal up
The war bright as roses in snow
Childhood will always lead you
By the hand that you have lost

Sprechen lernen

Dies ist ein Baum Baum dies hier
ein Teich Katze Mond und Sterne
fallen vom Baum in den Teich Teich
Dies war ein Haus hier war die Tür
hier stand ein Bett und dies hier

aus *Der Schnabelberg*

Learning to Speak

This is a tree tree this here
A pond cat moon and stars fall
From the tree into the pond pond
This was a house here was the door
Here stood a bed and this here

Stufen

Jetzt weiß das Kind wie man schläft
es hat seine Sinne vergessen
die Mutter auf Strümpfen hinaus

Alles ist zu lernen Geduld Warten
auch die größte Liebe zieht einmal
das Messer aus meiner Brust

Beruhigend mein Leben
es wird nicht gehen ehe ich weiß
wie man richtig gestorben ist

aus *Der Schnabelberg*

Steps

Now the child knows how to sleep
It has forgotten its senses
The mother creeps out on stockinged feet

So much to be learned patience waiting
Even the love of my life will one day
Draw the dagger from my breast

Reassuring that my life
Won't leave until I know
How one dies properly

Wirklichkeit

Nah ist mir das trockene Holz unter
der Hand Brückengeländer das
meine Kindheit mit der Stadt verband
nah ist mir wie der Wind die
Schwalbe in den Augenwinkel küßt
sie auf Händen trägt durch alle Luft
nah ganz nah sind mir Arm Schulter die
Wange des Geliebten den ich nie sehe
zuinnerst alles was ich entbehre

Meine Träume stehen Rücken zur Wand
zählen mit wie die Welle steigt
da sagt mir gestern ein Freund:
Ich weiß nicht wann der Augenblick des
Glücks kommen wird aber ich erwarte ihn

aus *Der Schnabelberg*

Reality

Dear to me is the feel of dry wood beneath
My hand the parapet of a bridge that
Linked my childhood with the town
Dear to me is the way the wind kisses
The swallow in the corner of its eye
Carries it oh so carefully through the air
Dear very dear to me are the arm shoulder
Cheek of my beloved whom I never see
Deep down everything I do without

My dreams stand with their backs to the wall
Counting along as the wave rises
Then a friend said to me yesterday:
I don't know when the moment of
Happiness will arrive but I'm waiting for it

aus
Ortswechsel des Herzens

from
Heart Changing Places

Orpheus, weiblich

für dich würde ich mich,
würde mich einkaufen beim
guten oder bösen vielleicht
Hirten Richter Kommandanten,
mit meiner Stimme würde ich
wenn er das Lösegeld zählt
sagen ich habe den Berg versetzt,
dich loskaufen, herauslösen
bis meine Zunge bricht, die
Stimme müßte das tun die du
immer anders hörst als ich

aus *Ortswechsel des Herzens*

Orpheus, Feminine

For you I would sell my,
would sell my self go
to the good or even the bad
shepherd judge commandant,
I would use my voice
to say I have moved mountains
as he counts out the ransom,
would set you free, set you loose
until my tongue breaks, my voice
would do that my voice which you
always hear differently from me

Weiterleben

ohne dich würde ich weiter
leben ohne dich bis es,
weiter leben wie bevor du,
lebt es so lang hat Augen
wie zuvor hat Blicke gleich,
geht es mir ohne dich wie es
mir geht läuft fällt, wäre ich
abgezogen mit ganzer Haut recht
kalt, lebt es hält es mich fest
was kam kommt einmal kommt: kopf-
über hinunterfliegen in
die Umarmung des Gehsteigs

aus *Ortswechsel des Herzens*

Carrying on Living

Without you I would carry
on living without you until,
carry on living like before you,
living that long having eyes
like before look just the same
get along without you just as
I get along run fall, I would be
so cold with my skin peeled
off, living holding me there
what came comes once will come:
flying head-over into
the embrace of the pavement

Missing child

1

Die Zeugen kommen nicht mehr
jeden Tag, die mein Kind
gesehen haben wollen.
Auf dem Bild, das der Computer
altern lassen kann, erkenne
ich es selbst nicht mehr.
Ich warte nur noch auf den
fremden Erwachsenen, mir so
vertraut, daß er sagen kann:
du redest wie ein Kind.

2

Meine Freunde sind
Eltern von Kindern.
Das Leben weitergeben,
sagen sie, gibt auch
unserem Leben Sinn.
Ich trage meine Krankheit
in mir, als den sicheren
Tod meines Kindes, das
nie gelebt hat.
Diese Genügsamkeit macht
mich schon manchen fremd.

3

Die Lippen kurz berührt
wie auf der Flucht, dann
besinnst du dich, niemand
stört uns, trennt uns.
Im Nebenzimmer blättert
das Kind um, das wir
nicht haben.

aus *Ortswechsel des Herzens*

Missing Child

1

The witnesses no longer come
every day, claiming
to have seen my child.
In the picture that the computer
can make age I no longer
recognise it myself.
I'm just waiting for the
adult stranger, so very
familiar, that he can say:
you're talking like a child.

2

My friends are
parents to children.
Passing on life,
they say, also gives
our lives meaning.
I carry my illness
inside of me, as the certain
death of my child who
has never lived.
This unassuming modesty
seems strange to some.

3

Lips brushed briefly
as if on the run, then
you remember, no one
will disturb us, separate us.
In the next room the child
we don't have turns
the page.

from *Heart Changing Places*

aus *Septemtriones*

I

Keine Träne aus dem See geschöpft
hielt dein verirrter Blick für
Stunden an mir fest und lag ich
wars ein Boot bei dir stahl
mit der dunklen einer Stimme
deiner Nacht mich aus dem Licht
in dem dein Lebewohl sich färbt.

IX

Ich war noch blind ich sah
den grauen See ein weißes Haus
den schwarzen Tisch an dem ich
später mich so zugeneigt und jedes
Wort verstand ich war noch schuld-
los unterwegs als ich zum letzten Mal
so leichten Herzens dich begrüßt.

XII

Links die Welt und rechts mein
Wort es schließt das Pfauen-
auge Nacht sagt: bleib! bleibt
atmend blau auf blau wie heimlich
kunstvoll zugefügt wie dieses
du bleib hier du halte still
nicht ahnend wo die Zeile schließt.

aus *Ortswechsel des Herzens*

from *Septemtriones*

I

Not even a tear fished from the lake
your wandering gaze would fix
on me for hours and I was lying
was it like a boat beside you
stole with the dark voice of your
night out of the morning
which is colouring your farewell.

IX

I was still blind I saw
the grey lake a white house
the black table at which I sat so
fondly next to you and understood
each single word I was still guilt-
less on my way when I one last
time greeted you light-heartedly.

XII

To the left the world to the right
my word it shuts the peacock
eye of night says: stay stays
breathing blue on blue like it has been
accomplished skilfully in secret like this
will you stay here will you hold still
not guessing where the line will end.

from *Heart Changing Places*   153

XIII

Schreibt jeden Tag sie ein
Gedicht das ist als ob der See
den Berg erträgt die sanfte
schwere Zeichnung in der Haut
das ist als ob der See den Berg
sich holen will der manchmal
zärtlich Steine schickt.

XXVI

Eine Handvoll Wörter immer nur mit
denen ich dich hungrighalten will
mein Raubtier Pranken größer als
mein Herz – so wär ich gern gefangen
Krallen Gitterstäbe sanft gesetzt mit
jedem Herzschlag stoßend an dein
bleib bei mir.

XXXIII

Es bleibt wir bleiben weit und
schicken Gründe hin und her so
heimlich gut ein Netz auf dem
ich näher nachts in deinen Traum
ach du ich sag dir nur und schlaf:
mein Nußbaum atmet tief von
seinen schweren Krähen auf.

XXXIX

Mein Herz schlägt fest nach
mir mit seinem sanften Huf es
treibt was mich auch treibt und
schneller liebt so liebt so liebt
und überholt dies Sehnen mich was
sag ich dir dann herz- und atem-
los ich kenn du kennst mich nicht.

aus *Ortswechsel des Herzens*

XIII

If every day she writes
a poem it is as if the lake
can bear the mountain the soft
deep markings in the skin
it is as if the lake will fetch
the mountain which sometimes
tenderly sends stones.

XXVI

Only a handful of words each time
for me to keep you hungry
my predator paws bigger than
my heart – that's how I'd like to be
encaged claws padded bars with
every heartbeat running into your
stay with me.

XXXIII

That's it we'll stay away and
we'll send reasons back and forth
a secretly good net on which I
creep up closer to your dream at night:
oh love is all I say to you and sleep:
my walnut tree can breathe again
freed from its heavy weight of crows.

XXXIX

My heart is beating after me
beats with its gentle muffled hooves
it's driven by what drives me too
and loves more quickly loves so loves
and if this longing overtakes me what
will I say then so heart- and breath-
less that I know you do not know me.

from *Heart Changing Places*   155

LVII

Auf Ausschau blind ist jetzt der See in
den der Regen fein mit tausend Nadeln
sticht kein Berg kein Bild ganz in sich
selbst versunken trüb kreist er nur um sein
eignes Leid und möchte härten seine Haut –
und überhört was ihm der Berg verspricht:
ich geh in dir als Donner heut zur Ruh.

LXIII

Was führst du sag mit mir im Schild
wenn nun mein Blick dir diesen Stein
verwandelt in dein Herz zurück? wen
wirst du lieben? wem verschweigen
daß du dann so spät nochmals das Haus
verläßt und mir mit deiner weichen
Hand die Lider schließt?

LXVI

Du hast gefragt was wünschst du
dir es fiel mir nach dem Abschied
ein: wär's denkbar daß ich lauf dem
Amokschützen ins Geheg von dem du
abends mir erzählt? der Wahnsinns-
tat die meine Liebe blutsverwandt
umfängt?

LXVII

Als ich vor dir stand nach dem
Bad dir alle meine Blößen gab
die Schenkel mürb die Hüften auf-
geschwemmt traf mich dein Blick –
traf die Attrappe wo die Krankheit
täglich übt für ihren Sieg war ich
versöhnt in dir mit meinem Krieg.

aus *Ortswechsel des Herzens*

LVII

On lookout now the lake is blind
a fine rain falls in it a thousand needles
no mountain no image immersed
in contemplation of itself it broods
on its own sorrow anxious to toughen up its skin –
and does not hear the promise of the mountain:
This day I come to rest in you as thunder.

LXIII

Tell me what you have in mind for me
when one glance from the shield can turn
this stone back into your heart? Who
will you love? From whom conceal
how you then leave the house again
so late and close my eyelids
with your gentle hand?

LXVI

You asked me what I wanted but
it struck me after everyone had
gone: is it conceivable that I might
run into the crazy gunman you were
telling me about that night? The insane
deed encompassing my love as if it
were a blood relation?

LXVII

When I stood before you after my
bath and showed you all my nakedness
thighs sagging hips bloated
your gaze fell on my body –
fell on this dummy where an illness
rehearses daily for its triumph and I
was reconciled with my old war in you.

from *Heart Changing Places*   157

Welcher deiner vielen Briefe –
der in dem du mir für alles dankst?
Welches süßbesiegte Weigern? Als
du diesen einen Tag noch bliebst?
Welcher Finger? Wieviel Strähnen?
Ich möcht mich manchmal töten weil
du mich dann nicht vergißt.

aus *Ortswechsel des Herzens*

LXXIX

Which of your many letters –
the one in which you thank me for it all?
Which sweetly overcome refusal? The time
you stayed behind that day?
Which finger? How many strands of hair?
I sometimes want to kill myself so
you will then remember me.

A Conversation with Evelyn Schlag

Beverley Driver Eddy

The following conversation took place on 7 November 2001, during Evelyn Schlag's month-long stay in Carlisle, Pennsylvania, as Dickinson College's Max Kade Writer-in-Residence. A longer version of this interview was originally published in PN Review 146 *(July–August 2002). Beverley Driver Eddy is the editor of* Evelyn Schlag: Readings of Text *(Bern and New York: Peter Lang, 2004).*

BDE: May I start by asking you whether you think poetry has a function in today's society?

ES: I think what I associate with writing has been influenced by the reason I learned to write. Now, obviously you learn to write because you simply have to. In my case, I was five and pre-school. My parents were in New York for a year. This was 1957. My father was an intern in a hospital and tried to pick up as much about anaesthesiology as possible, because at the time there were no trained anaesthesiologists in Austria. He watched the birth of Caroline Kennedy from the third row. Meantime I was staying with my grandparents in their home; they lived on the first floor, we on the second, so it wasn't much of a move. But I missed my mother terribly and wanted to write to her. So my grandfather taught me, and I wrote on the back of the many photographs that he took of me, chronicling my growing up, usually with a cat in my arms. So in my mind writing has always been associated with longing, and with what you call *herbeischreiben* in German – not only imagining very vividly and conjuring up the presence of my mother while I was writing to her, but also effecting her return, and not by asking her to come home soon, but by the power of language. The words that I set on those postcards in capital letters had a power of their own. They were magic. I still believe in the power of love poems. I still want to prove Auden wrong, that poetry *does* make something happen.

Your grandfather features quite often in your poems.

He was a wonderful man. A very handsome, melancholy man who had been forced to take over his father's shop – selling leather, little wooden nails, lots of little things the farmers would buy when they came down from their villages on market day. As a child I used to

161

sit at his desk hidden by the suitcases that were piled up and listen in on peoples' stories. I liked to write things down and run the blotting cradle over the words so the ink would get soaked up. He was an avid reader, he'd sit there at the table, cigarette between his slender fingers, like one of those 1950s actors in the programmes you got in the cinema. He died when I was six.

When did you first know you were going to be a writer?

Actually in secondary grammar school, when I was seventeen, we had somebody come from Vienna who tried to give us some counselling about jobs (*Berufsberatung*). I cannot remember any of the questions we had to answer on those yellow sheets (which looked old even then) or how they tried to find out about our talents, but I know we had to give our 'dream job' and the job we thought we would likely end up with. For my dream job I wrote 'writer', and for the other one 'editor'. I began writing poems when I was in Vienna, studying German and English literature. I had a wonderful Polish teacher at university who encouraged me to write. Another professor actually set the direction for me when he learned that I had won a prize in a literary competition. I had written a fairly surrealistic text about Felix Austria. He congratulated me on the prize and said, 'Why don't you become a writer?' He may have had second thoughts about my academic career; I was already doing work on my dissertation about presentation of women characters in contemporary English and American novels.

Did you ever finish that?

No. I started teaching part-time and began to write seriously. My first book was a short novel called *Nachhilfe* (*Tuition*, 1981) about a woman who engages a private tutor for her kids and learns some lessons about life herself.

It seems to me that one of your favourite themes in your prose writing is how people unexpectedly meet and make something miraculous out of this encounter, teaching each other to see the world differently. It comes up again and again. Another theme that occurs quite frequently, in both your prose and your poetry, is illness.

Well, with a doctor for a father you may be predisposed for certain fields of interest. I have had a chronic disease (diabetes) since I was thirteen, which pretty much influences a lot of what I am doing. I also had tuberculosis twice, and that accounts for my love for Katherine Mansfield as a writer and as a person.

I wonder if you could speak a little about your experimentation with form. For instance, in the section of Ortswechsel des Herzens[1]

1 *Ortswechsel des Herzens* (Frankfurt am Main: S. Fischer Verlag, 1989).

entitled 'Orpheus, weiblich' ('Orpheus, Feminine') I noticed you used punctuation as you had in your previous volume,[2] while in 'Septemtriones' you didn't, but worked instead with fixed stanzas.

I did use punctuation in the beginning, yes. But the thing about punctuation is that I just don't like interruptions. I have poems where I use punctuation, but these tend to be more narrative poems. I like to keep lines running on, you know, I don't like lines to be that fixed at the end.

Tell me about 'Septemtriones'.

The term is made up. 'Septemtriones' means 'seven stars'. When I started writing these poems I didn't know, of course, that there would be so many of them. They started out as six-line poems or eight-line poems, but not longer. So I thought, since the number seven is something magical, I would write them in seven-line stanzas, but in a very open form. That is, I would use some internal rhyme wherever it could be managed, and also, since there are eighty-four poems (again a number that's divisible by seven), I would give it an arrangement something like a constellation, because it is a constellation of two figures, two persons, two characters. There is a poem at the beginning that is not written by me, that was written by the person to whom these poems were addressed, that is just signed 'K' and I don't refer to more specifically than stars in a constellation.

In 'Versuchungen'[3] ('Temptations'), you turn from internal rhyme to end rhyme, and write sonnets.

Yes. Although I don't like sonnets.

Did you decide that only after you wrote them?

No, the thing that got me going was that I had translated Douglas Dunn's poems, and so I decided I just had to get used to sonnets, to work with them. And I thought, why not try it myself? Of course I had read lots of sonnets, but never with the intention of writing one. And since then, I haven't used this form much. I really don't like it a lot, because it goes along too much with one's expectations. It's just too predictable for me.

Is [the rhyme scheme] part of what bothers you about sonnets in terms of predictability?

Yes, but then again, it's exactly the rhyme scheme and what you have to do that makes you come up with words that you'd never have thought of. This is the thing that might turn something predictable into something very original. And then – I moved away

2 *Einflüsterung nahe seinem Ohr* (Vienna: Edition Maioli zu Wien, 1984).
3 From *Der Schnabelberg* (Frankfurt am Main: S. Fischer Verlag, 1992).

to more narrative poems, but I tended to dislike them, too, because I think they can be too open in a way, too blunt. And then I have also written other kinds of poems, I've written short poems, in a very dense language.

I've always liked very short, very lyrical poems. That sort of poem generally hasn't had very good press, lately, but I've always written them. They tend to be less accessible, of course. One reason is that I use a lot of images that are – syntactically – open at both ends. You can connect to the sentence preceding as well as to the one following. I don't do that much anymore. Although I'd hope that there will still be readers who just surrender themselves to that particular kind of poetical language and let themselves get carried away word by word, because they are not arbitrarily placed, they do have a logical sequence.

How did you develop this style of poetry? Were you influenced by any particular poets?

I think if there was a poet who influenced me at the time I started writing poetry it was Ilse Aichinger. I like the way she was always looking for the simple words, you know, *einfache Wörter, schlichte Wörter, die schlechten Wörter* ['simple words, plain words, poor words'] – but at the same time her words were obscure.

Are there any special techniques you employ to achieve this combination of simplicity and obscurity?

One that I employ – not always consciously at first – is *taking words literally*. Since there is an abundance of idioms in German that work with physical images, this often makes sensual sense of words. In my poem 'Fischblut' ('Fish Blood')[4] for example, what you would associate with the words *fish blood* would be its metaphorical meaning; you would expect a poem about somebody very cold and reckless, and in fact it turns out that there is such a character in the poem, but, at the same time, it means the actual blood of a fish. The speaker is a female fish who follows the voice of her seducer upstream, and this following upstream, while it clearly relates to the salmon's wanderings (even though the fish is not a salmon), also makes use of the idiom *jemanden in seinen Strom ziehen*, 'to draw somebody into one's stream or current'. The female fish, the female lover, the woman, ends up in a smokehouse, so her fish blood gets dried up, and at the same time the man who has lured her upstream has shown he is a fish-blooded character.

Of course this makes for a poetry that is not easy to translate,

---

4 From *Das Talent meiner Frau* (Salzburg and Vienna: Residenz Verlag, 1999).

since it works so closely with the ambiguities and hidden meanings of the original language.

Do you think of this as something uniquely German?

I think that this way of using the German language at several levels is something very characteristically Austrian. There is a double meaning to a lot of things we say. Our daily language is very often one of wordplay, much more so I think than with Germans. There is a subversive power in the way Austrians use language, because very often we have that underdog feeling vis-à-vis a German German-speaker.

The syntax in 'Orpheus, weiblich' is difficult in spite of the punctuation in these poems.

Well, you see, quite a few of the poems in that sequence deal with the possibility of loss of a beloved person and its consequences. They are syntactically disrupted, the syntax mirrors the shattering. In the first poem of the sequence, for example, I begin with '*Für dich würde ich mich*' – 'For you I would'. Sentences get cut off, words get stuck before they can be uttered. '*Die Umarmung des Gehsteigs*' – 'the embrace of the pavement' – I want this to be felt by the reader, how the pavement approaches you when you fling yourself out of the window and finally embraces you with its concrete arms.

More recently my poems have become more accessible syntaxwise. This has a lot to do with reading so much American and English poetry – Louise Glück, to mention one. And Elizabeth Bishop.

In your latest published volume, Das Talent meiner Frau *(1999), you have a sequence of war poems. This is a theme quite new to your work.*

I was inspired, of course, by the wars in Yugoslavia. I was in Belgrade when the whole thing began, when Milosevic came to power in 1989. There was a literary conference, and writers from all over the world were invited. The strange thing was that the subject of that conference was 'Heroic epics'. All the writers were wondering, who would do that now? I remember talking to a Dutch writer and asking, 'Have you encountered a heroic epic recently that really matters to you?' But the Serbian writers went on and on about sublimation, and we got parts of these poems translated, and I couldn't believe my ears, because at the time – this was 1989 – they had had this anniversary of the colossal battle on the Amselfeld.[5] That's when the whole war propaganda started, and of course nobody knew what it would lead to. It was actually

5 Where the Serbians were defeated by the Ottoman Turks on 28 June 1389.

the beginning of a new kind of nationalism, and the strange thing was that writers and intellectuals and journalists would join to a high degree.

And of course the wars were really quite close to where I live. At one point there was actually some firing across the border when Slovenia was the first state to become independent. It was a rather quick affair, fortunately.

In ['Laura's Songs' and 'Summer Elegies'] you seem to be continuing your interest in experimentation with forms and syntax.

Yes, these are two very different sequences. With Laura's poems, I first invented poems, in a way, and then I invented a poet who had written them – a poet called Laura; the protagonist in a novel that I finished recently. And these are very simple poems that I think could be set to music. They are basically four-line stanzas that do not rhyme; they seem like sixteenth-century songs.

I think the Laura poems are a sort of a mask, really, although they're very autobiographical, as well. But they give me a very strong sense of having a persona. And I can invest her with as much of my biography as I want to, and I can make her do things that I wouldn't do.

The 'Summer Elegies' appear to be more personal.

The 'Summer Elegies' are very autobiographical poems. They are a sequence of seventeen poems of different length, of different form. I wrote them over two years or so, mostly in the summer of 1999. Initially the title was going to be 'The Summer That Was Ages Too Short', but my English publisher suggested I change it to 'Summer Elegies'. They are dedicated to my husband.

What makes them elegies?

They are elegies both for the summer of 1999 and for a friend of mine who died during that summer. It was the summer of the solar eclipse, which was very visible in the part of Austria where I live. And it was a very strong experience. Very recently they have become elegies in an unforeseeable way. My husband and I rented a wonderful farm for twenty years. It was actually a manor house with a large park, beautiful old trees. I used to spend summers there writing. The place taught me most of what I know about nature. The lease has not been renewed. The trees have been cut down.

I like the way they are imbued with awareness of time passing even as you capture the moment, of holding fast to certain seconds and realising they are passing, too.

Yes. Certainly when you get older you cherish time more, with each day. And the Elegies are really also for the summer – the summer of life.

In these elegies, too, you have a tremendous variety of settings. Had you gone to all those places that summer?

We had been to Ferrara, but the trip to the Czech Republic was an earlier memory. We went there, my husband and I and a friend – actually the friend who provided me with a lot of material about the Baroque writer Catharina Regina von Greiffenberg[6] – and we went to this little place to the north of Austria beyond the border in the Czech Republic, because, for one thing it's the birthplace of the Austrian writer Adalbert Stifter, and for the other, there was a gorgeous view down this valley where the Vltava – the Moldau – flows, and where part of the valley is flooded, so the path of the old river only shows when it's freezing. When it's very cold and when all the water freezes, it somehow freezes in a different white. But it's still difficult to make out the lines, we were standing there for a very long time willing ourselves to see it. And then we thought we did, and I took dozens of photographs. The reason why I mention this Baroque writer, Catharina Regina von Greiffenberg, is that she was a very religious writer, and she believed that God was showing up in nature, so that we could read it and find signs from God. And I thought this was something she would have liked very much, you know, it was a very strange and strong sign.

Is this a point of identification between you and the Baroque poet?

I think so, yes. I may in fact be a very 'religious' writer, not in any confessional way, but in the sense that I keep reading nature for signs, and conceive of natural phenomena as emanations from – whom? But I seem to be more interested in the message than the sender. What I want to say is that *anthropomorphism* for me is not only a technique, but very much my outlook on the world. For one thing it makes communication with the seemingly mute easier. It makes you a good listener. Of course, most writers are good listeners, because they are always out for stories. Attributing human qualities to seemingly inanimate things – one might say that it is either a very primitive way of colonising the material world, or else that it is a very naïve and childlike point of view. I think it is a rich source, and anyway it's second nature to me. Elegy XII says at the end: 'In the oven the logs settle themselves / They give off little sounds of relief.' Or in Elegy XIII, which is all about the sense of hearing and ultimately the fear of becoming deaf, the car 'stalks its way across the gravel'.

---

6 For her story 'Die lustwählende Schäferin' ('The Hedonistic Shepherdess'), from her collection *Unsichtbare Frauen* (*Invisible Women*; Salzburg and Vienna: Residenz Verlag, 1995).

Would you call the Elegies confessional poems?

Not with the reputation that the confessional poem nowadays has, which is a very bad one. I think the term has suffered from too much feminist theory being connected with it. Nowadays I think you would associate the confessional poem with a woman moved to write herself into – not into the mainstream, but into some kind of accepted poetry by women.

On the other hand, a writer always confesses. The moment you use language, you confess. I guess I dislike the term *confessional*, because, and this may have to do with my own Catholic upbringing, it implies confessing sin. Now, I'm not confessing sin, I'm being truthful, I try to make my language as truthful as is possible.

I find the whole treatment of landscape in your poems to be especially striking, in that you incorporate nature in ways that create inescapable images. Yet, in Elegy VIII, you seem to question your ability to do this.

What created this poem was in fact the line 'That first winter in Wiltshire' which is from a poem by Elaine Feinstein, and it struck me when I was reading that poem that I saw the landscape immediately, even though I hadn't been there, and I thought that this English landscape was just so big and so important and so charged. And then I compared it to what would happen if I wrote 'that first winter in —' and then filled in some of my places. And that set off a kind of meditation about how I have been watching my landscapes for so many years now, and I do this very intensely and purposefully. So I go places a hundred times and pass certain routes over the hills. The poem is broken up into two pieces, with my husband answering. It's a poem about patience, it's about how long it takes to learn to read the landscape, to read a person.

So we're back to time again…

Sure. It's very much about time. But it sees time in a very positive way, because it's sort of a consolation, that there is always something more to learn about somebody you think you know, a landscape you know.